Jesus Politics:
The Four Gospels in Politics

Tony Franklin

Parson's Porch

Book Publishing

Jesus Politics: The Four Gospels in Politics
ISBN: Softcover 978-1-949888-48-5
Copyright © 2017 by Tony Franklin

To order additional copies of this book, contact:

Parson's Porch Books
1-423-475-7308
www.parsonsporch.com

Parson's Porch Books is an imprint of **Parson's Porch & Book Publishers** in Cleveland, Tennessee, which has double focus. We focus on the needs of creative writers who need a professional publisher to get their work to market, **&** we also focus on the needs of others by sharing our profits with those who struggle in poverty to meet their basic needs of food, clothing, shelter and safety.

Jesus Politics:
The Four Gospels in Politics

Special Thanks to:

Dr. John Hurtgen who inspired me to write this book,

Shannon Blosser for research help,

John, Mike, Eric, Fella, Iosmar, and Larry and those who read and
encouraged me to publish,

my awesome editor Mandy Mowers,

and my wife Bekah and family for giving me the time and space to
put this together.

This book is dedicated to all who have the courage to stand up and lead with the Character and Spirit of Jesus Christ.

Contents

Chapter One...11

    Preliminary: What are the Gospels Anyway?

Chapter Two 17

    The Politics of Getting to Jesus

Chapter Three..29

    The Pharisees and the Gospel of Matthew

Chapter Four..49

    The Zealots and the Gospel of Mark

Chapter Five...72

    The Sadducees and The Gospel of Luke-Acts

Chapter Six 97

    The Essenes and the Gospel of John

Chapter Seven 131

    Conclusions

Chapter One
Preliminary: What are the Gospels Anyway?

Introduction and Outline

Who am I?

The first president of the United States that I can remember in office was Ronald Reagan. In first grade, George H. W. Bush, was campaigning for the presidency against Michael Dukakis. I remember doing a mock vote in our class for who should win the presidency in our small-town elementary school in rural Illinois. If memory serves correctly, Michael Dukakis won with about two-thirds of our classroom.

In 1999 and 2000 I joined my high school speech team and was given the topic of campaign finance reform. The last time I had really paid attention to politics was the previous decade in that first grade mock election. The research I did was disheartening as I began to uncover some of the underhanded and corrupt things done with money in our political system. In addition to that, I was very much a part of the hormone-driven, angst-filled grunge culture that was sweeping our nation among late Gen-Xers and early Millennials during the end of the last century. The whole experience was disheartening and made me want to be done with politics for good.

During those years I can vaguely remember watching some of the Republican candidates debate and being impressed by a man named Alan Keyes. He stood out at the time as being an African-American candidate, and, although I did not know at the time he was Catholic, I did sense I kind of refreshing honesty and straightforwardness to his questions and answers in those debates. If I had been old enough to vote at the time, I probably would have voted for him. I knew very little about him personally and have not kept up with him over the years other than his brief attempt to run against Obama for one of the Illinois Senate seats. While he did not make it into the final rounds campaigning for the presidency, he did restore a little of my faith in our politics.

Politics ultimately could not help me, nor could the grunge culture I was following, and, midway through my junior year of high school,[1] I turned and sought help from the very God, Christ, and Church I was rebelling against. I have repeated that process every day and this book is just another small expression of that process.

Why this book?

The world has changed much since Ronald Reagan was president. The common cultural trend of keeping religion and politics in separate boxes has ended. Separation of church and state, while historic, has been argued, ignored, and changed in emphasis multiple times to suit our own agendas. The idea that you can maintain separation of church and state simply by forbidding the public support of any given candidate is not keeping the church out of politics, it is simply forcing the church to be non-partisan. The church has pushed a political agenda through specific issues since the beginning, and especially in more recent times around issues of civil rights, global relations, economic issues, and marriage.

In our recent campaign between Hillary Clinton and Donald Trump for the presidency, I imagine they were asked about their church affiliations and spiritual beliefs dozens of times each day. I believe that this is just another witness to the truth that spiritual beliefs and political beliefs are intertwined with all our other beliefs we have as human beings. Life is not simply set apart in separate boxes that never intersect. I believe life is much like a river that flows past many different banks, each affected by those that come before and after them — as well as outside influences. The growth of interconnectivity and integration between all areas of our lives has the effect of making us both more diverse and more connected than ever before and this interconnectivity has proven to be one of the greatest challenges of our generation.

---

[1] Very reminiscent of the opening of Dante's <u>Inferno</u> — "Midway upon the journey of our life I found myself within a forest dark, for the straightforward pathway had been lost."

We now live in a post-modern, pluralistic culture that has much in common with the Apostolic Age when the gospels were written and the Church was multiplying in the midst of many birth pains. Throughout much of history, faith and politics went hand in hand, though the particular relationship between the two varied from culture to culture, much as they do today. Today there is a new emphasis in interpreting the Bible for our context and applying the lessons we learn to our own cultures. The church has always pursued this interpretive work — this is nothing new. What has changed is the way we often do it today with a sense of enthusiastic literalism — believing what worked in Acts chapter 2 and 3 will work the same way for us today. I think, if we are honest, we are all just looking for some stability and honest answers in the face of the chaos and confusion we see every day.

This book is written specifically to look at some of the faith-full political values of the New Testament and how these new Christian values were used to guide some of the first generations of Christians in navigating the muddy political waters of their day, and perhaps how they may give us some guidance today as well.

What is a gospel?

The Gospels, by their very name, have been about politics from the moment they were created. The brief translation of the Greek word *euangelion* (the root of our word "gospel") is — "good news"[2]. It is an announcement to the public meant to bring joy and excitement. The traditional usage of the word in the Roman Empire was to announce the reign of a new ruler — either by birth or by conquest. When Rome conquered other nations, they would send military parades into towns with proclamations of "good news," that the fighting was over and that these people were going to be part of the Roman Empire.

Understandably, that was not always taken as good news for the conquered people. To them, it may very well have seemed the opposite of "good news." However, the writers of the Gospels in

---

[2] Word derived from the Anglo-Saxon *godspell* denoting "glad tidings" or "good news." Elwell, W. A., & Beitzel, B. J. (1988). In Baker encyclopedia of the Bible (p. 892). Grand Rapids, MI: Baker Book House.

the New Testament used this same term to denote Christ's birth and conquest of the world. Like the Roman proclamations, not everyone took this to be "good news." Chief among the examples of this is King Herod, portrayed in Matthew and Luke, whose own reign, according to the narrative, is threatened by the birth of Jesus and who sends soldiers out to kill innocent children in a mad attempt to crush this rival to the throne and to the hearts of Israel. For Herod, an unfaithful ruler of the Jews, the Gospel of Christ was not good news at all.

I suppose your own response to the Gospels, the good news of Jesus Christ, depends on your particular position. For those in power, particularly when that power is under-girded and maintained by means contrary to the will of God, the Gospels are a challenge and perhaps a threat. However, those who are oppressed by such power and who have built their lives trusting in God will find release, redemption, and joy in the light of this King of kings who will reign forever and ever.

Thesis

In John 14:6, Jesus claimed to be "the Way, the Truth, and the Life" and that no one came to the Heavenly Father without Him. I believe that. Jesus did *not* run for office back in the first century AD nor is He running now. He is both the end result we seek as well as the way we will get there. The problem is not finding the right end result. The problem is finding the path from where we stand.

Unlike teachers such as Aristotle and Plato, we do not have a book from Jesus about his thoughts on politics. While his teachings from the Gospels occasionally delve into the subject of politics, much of it is interwoven with many other subjects as well. Often our best work uncovering political values has been using the parables and teachings of Jesus as analogies to be translated into present political values. There is value in that kind of work, but there is more that can be uncovered if we look deeper into the political context that serves as the backdrop of the Gospels and begin to see the words and deeds of Jesus as a response to those political challenges.

The Jews of the New Testament had undergone leadership changes and challenges for thousands of years before Jesus was born, and one of the problems Jesus faced in His ministry was that not all Jews thought alike. There were at least four distinct types of Jews, each divided along interpretations of the Scriptures and how to apply them to their faith and politics. Each of the four Gospels bears some distinguishing ways of telling the same good news that uniquely spoke to those four dynamics at work in Israel.

I also believe that we still have these four distinctive groups, divided by political and faith values today, though they bear different names. It is my hope that a return to these political values, found in each of the four Gospels will lead us as communities of faith, as a nation, and as a world, back to Jesus — the Way, the Truth, and the Life.

Outline: Where we are going?

The setup of this book is fairly direct. We begin with a very brief overview of the politics of the Jews throughout the course of their cultural history. I will show how these four different types of Jews were created. Chapters 2-5 will begin with Matthew and follow the Gospels in canonical order. Each of these chapters begins with an explanation of a primary political value of the Jewish group and ends with a political value Jesus presents in that Gospel to challenge the initial value.

Within these four chapters, the pairing of Jewish demographic and gospel is entirely arbitrary. The gospels were written to a variety of audiences, some of them not Jewish at all. It should not be expected that the Gospel of Matthew, for example, was written specifically to the Pharisees. However, there is material in Matthew that would have challenged the Pharisees of the first century and our own time as well.

Chapter 6 will conclude with some thoughts about how to use this information to help us best assess our present communities and give them the best guidance from all four gospels to help us align our faith and politics with the Way that Jesus has given us. By the end of this book, you will know four distinctly Christian values regarding the relationship between faith and politics, have the Scripture to describe their foundation, and understand some historical examples in which they have been used by others to follow Christ as they changed the world around them.

Chapter Two
The Politics of Getting to Jesus
The History of Hebrew Authority

Moses

The history of Hebrew spiritual and political authority finds its origin in the man called Moses. Not only are the first books of the Bible named after him (The Law of Moses) and probably written or dictated by him, he was the first to call the Hebrew people to live together as a national community rather than as individual tribal families. Around 1300 BC Moses began the longstanding tradition of leading the people of God like a shepherd through the wilderness for 40 years.

Moses never referred to Scripture to support his authority, some of which was first being written during his lifetime. Instead, he referred to the past experiences the people had with God. This became part of the prophetic tradition, particularly looking back to the parting of the Red Sea and the defeat of the Egyptian Army. Since there was no written text and God sometimes spoke to him alone on behalf of the people, Moses became the sole authority of the Hebrew people. Only his brother Aaron could claim a bit of authority as chief priest of the people, although that authority may arguably be due to his relationship with Moses.

All issues of justice and law interpretation came directly to Moses. We know this because the Scripture tells us it became a problem. Jethro, Moses' father-in-law, counseled him to appoint lesser judges among the tribes to help delegate the issues of justice among the people in order to allow Moses the freedom to lead.[3] The way Scripture identifies this problem is just further evidence of the extreme authority that Moses had over the people. In this time before scripture was written and accessible to the people, the point of authority was focused instead on an individual person who displayed evidence of God's power.

---

[3] Exodus 18:13-27

Moses

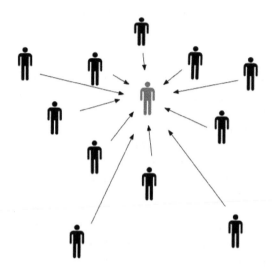

David

The society, culture, and government of the Hebrew people were transformed when they finally settled in the Promised Land. The slight tension of authority that existed between Moses as head prophet and Aaron as head priest began to grow and expand. Joshua, who took over after Moses began to lead the people, served not only as a prophet, but as something that would come to be called a *judge*, which designated a military and judicial authority as well as religious and political.

After nearly 300 years living in this tension, the people asked the last ruling prophet, Samuel, to establish a monarchy for them so that they might have a king like the other nations around them. He was an established prophet, but the people had come to distrust the authority of prophets and priests.[4] Samuel sought God's guidance in establishing a king reluctantly and thereby began the often-tragic

---

[4] See 1 Samuel 1

history of the kings of Israel. These culminated very quickly in the reign of King David and Solomon, and began crumbling apart in the generations that followed.

This move to a monarchy really just consecrated and gave official approval to the split in authority that had grown between the nation's head prophet, chief priest, and king. Each position was given particular privileges and powers to keep one another in a semblance of balance. The head prophet brought the word of God and was one of the only people who could exercise authority over the king without breaking protocol. If there were any accusations to be made against the king, they had to come from the head prophet. It was the prophet who chose and anointed the king, following God's will, and it was the prophet who would deliver the message if the king's authority had been taken away.

The chief priest was perhaps the weakest of these three persons of authority, but they were the only people allowed into the innermost sanctum of the temple, the Holy of Holies, to mediate on behalf of the nation of Israel before her God. It was the chief priest who personally dealt with the spiritual consequences of sin in the nation, and truly it was this person who began to base their authority on the interpretation of the scriptures. They could prescribe spiritual activities (based upon the scriptures) to all the people of Israel in order to obtain forgiveness and healing.[5]

The public point of judicial and military authority, taking on after the history of judges, was the king himself. The king became the most visible authority of the people, winning the hearts of the nation and wielding the widest and most immediate power over them. While their decisions were often guided by the prophets and they delegated the religious authority to the chief priest, it was the king who was the authority over the day-to-day workings of the nation.

One of the results of this division of authority between the single point found in Moses to these three persons in the time of King David was that each person in authority began to gather a faction of people around themselves. The king had his servants and soldiers who deferred to him. The chief priest had the other temple priests

[5] See Leviticus 8

and Levites who found their primary source of leadership in him. The head prophet began to gather disciples of their own who followed them above all others. This would fuel further distrust created in the political system that would very quickly fall apart in the face of the charges of government corruption and exploitation of servants in the time of King Solomon. In essence, the division of authority from one to three may have facilitated the eventual dissolution of the government of Israel.

David

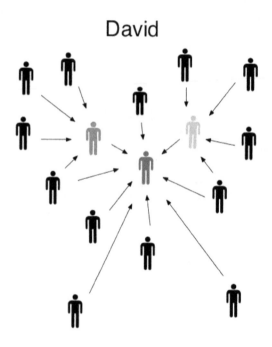

Time of Exile

The two biggest political influences that most affected the Hebrew people in the generations that followed King Solomon were distrust/breakdowns in the government of Israel in the first century following Solomon's reign (900-800 BC) and the experience of exile from their homeland to Babylon and Assyria in the centuries that followed. For those of us who have only experienced short visits out of the country for business or vacations, it is difficult to imagine the social violence that occurs when a people are uprooted from their homes and relocated at the whims of another nation. It has been some 300 years after the Native Americans experienced this and they are still profoundly affected by that experience.

In Israel, it began with the death of king Solomon. The elders came to the successor, Rehoboam, and asked if he would be more lenient with them than his father had been. Solomon had gathered great wealth and built many great buildings and monuments — including the Temple of God in Jerusalem, but he had done so with the work of the Jewish people. While it is not clear whether this was forced labor or if the people were simply working longer hours than they felt they could withstand, it is clear that the people were not getting wealthy themselves by building things for Solomon. To make matters worse, he was using people from all over the country, but it was primarily Jerusalem in the southern part of the nation that was enjoying the benefits of their labor. The northern tribes were fed up with this king who used them but was not caring for them. Rehoboam had a chance to reinforce the monarchy at that moment, but instead of being the shepherd to the people that the kings of Israel were supposed to be, he promised to be even harsher on the people than his father had been. That was the shot that started the civil war in Israel and precipitated their path into exile.

The kings that followed Rehoboam, both in the north (Israel) and the south (Judah) were a mixed bag of good and bad. According to the Old Testament accounts, most of these kings did not walk or rule in accordance with God's will for them, nor were the prophets that God sent to the people heeded. There were a few bright spots found in King Josiah and King Hezekiah, but neither king had the ability or faithfulness to turn the nation around and inspire faithfulness beyond their own generation. This erosion of Israelite monarchy further developed those factions that originated in the followers of the chief priest and head prophets and began to fragment even more under the rising threat of war from Assyria and Babylon — nations who were uniting and consuming the countries around them.

Eventually those nations swallowed up Northern Israel and Judah as well, and their fragmented authority shattered. Those in exile were given the choice to find their political authority in the king of their new country or face imprisonment and possibly death. The book of Daniel is an excellent example of the struggle it was for even the most faithful of the Jews (as they were renamed by the gentile nations during their exile) to remain faithful in their allegiance to God, let alone the former rulers of Israel. With their community scattered, it was every person for themselves. It was a long fall, but Israel eventually came to embrace that individualistic society of slavery from which Moses had attempted to free them almost 1000 years before. This nation of lost sheep had come full circle.

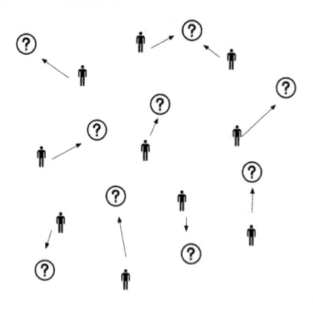

Formation under Occupation 1

The next several centuries gave birth to four distinct groups of Jews in Israel. While their experience in Exile varied from outright persecution to honor, sometimes under the same regime,[6] overall it was not a pleasant experience. Furthermore, the land of Israel and Jerusalem in particular lay in ruins. The Persians discovered that foreigners were more profitable to leave at home and tax rather than to recruit for slave labor, and so many Israelites were allowed to return home under the reign of Cyrus.[7] The Greeks followed suit and the Romans after them.

This final generation of Jews knew more of the political intrigues of the three or four nations who had inherited them than they knew of their own politics. That meant that their politics were created primarily as a response to the authority thrust upon them. They lived with the choice to rebel against that foreign authority or to submit

---

[6] See Daniel and Esther
[7] See Ezra and Nehemiah

to it each day. They had to weigh the consequences of rebellion or submission in deciding their own loyalty. There was enough frustration within the Jewish people to draw a line in the sand between those who were loyal to Rome and those who were not, and those two sides did not get along.

Formation under Occupation 2

Roman authority was not the only struggle the Jewish people dealt with, though. Over the centuries of exile, many Jewish people had lost touch with their culture. They no longer spoke the Hebrew language in ordinary life, but had traded that part of their culture in for Greek and Aramaic, which allowed them to conduct business among the nations. The Law of Moses had been lost and found several times, and their limited access to it in exile had resulted in the creation of the synagogue — a local place of worship in foreign lands, and a variety of interpretations of the Law of Moses in order to adapt to a foreign environment.

Most prominent among these varied interpretations were the disciples of Rabbi Hillel and Rabbi Shammai. Rabbi Hillel took a liberal approach to teaching the law, making it more practical and adaptable to those other cultures around them. Rabbi Shammai took the more conservative approach and sought to maintain a more literal interpretation of the law, even when it created hardships for those seeking to live by it. The Jewish council (Sanhedrin) often sided with Rabbi Hillel and elected him as their president. Although Hillel and Shammai rarely experienced strong disagreements themselves, their disciples were consistently at odds with one another. The Sanhedrin, seeing the value of both schools, adopted both and recognized there was a time and place for both value sets in their work interpreting the Law of Moses for a new millennium.[8]

This division between Hillel and Shammai worked its way into the culture of ordinary Jews. There were questions, not about whether to follow God or not, but how to do that on a practical, everyday level — and, in particular, how to interpret and apply the Law of Moses, their Holy Scripture. Some, like Shammai, considered it a

---

[8] See http://www.jewishvirtuallibrary.org/jsource/biography/hillel.html

part of their sacred heritage and wanted to take as strict and as literal an interpretation as possible. Others, recognizing and enjoying the fruit of interaction with other nations, sought to take a more liberal and big-picture approach to the Law of Moses — claiming they needed to follow the spirit of the law and the morals it taught rather than actually live out all of those commandments in every situation. Again, this division between the Jews would grow and solidify more and more with time.

Formation under Occupation 3

During the time of the New Testament, the Jews could find their identity by answering two questions:

1. What do you think about the Roman government?

2. What do you think about the Law of Moses?

Both were sources of authority in their lives, and, from time to time, these authorities would find themselves at odds with each other. That tension was lived out in the hearts and minds of the Jewish people on a daily basis.

Over time, the balance of beliefs in these two authorities split the Jews into four distinct types.

The way each group answered the questions regarding their reverence for God's law and their reverence for the ruling government put them each somewhere in a four-option matrix. It was easier to cope with the situation by aligning oneself with a particular group or set standard practice than thinking through every single scenario you came across yourself, and as the groups around these issues grew, so did their peer pressure and recruiting efforts. By the time Jesus began his ministry, most of these groups all had their own selected leaders, official uniforms, secret handshakes, etc. They had become official political entities in themselves carrying their own form of authority and those whose politics aligned with a particular group would have considered it an honor to officially join them.

The Four Types of Jews

Pharisees

The Pharisees are perhaps the best-known group of the Jews in the time of Jesus. They saw the Romans as a stumbling block to them as they sought to live out the Law of Moses in the best way possible. This motivation may have been backed by the idea that the Roman authority was thrust upon the Jews as a punishment for breaking the Law of Moses in generations past. Rome was the price they paid for their disobedience. While they did not expressly follow either Hillel or Shammai, they did not create excuses for those challenged by the Law of Moses. Instead, they took a new route of creating additional laws to sort of "build a hedge" around the Law of Moses. For example, in the Law of Moses the Third Commandment says, "Thou shalt not take the name of thy God in vain." To help ensure that rule was not broken, a new law was created that forbade the Jewish people from saying God's name at all, ever. You cannot take God's name if you do not say His name at all — or so they thought.

The Zealots

The Zealots hated the Roman government. Their relationship with the Law of Moses, though, is a bit misleading. They sought to end the tension of the Roman/Jewish authority by removing Rome from the equation using a military solution. Assassination was part of their stock and trade, and they had no sympathy for those who stood in their way. In other words, they expressly sought a political solution to a problem that was both political and religious in nature. In our country today, they would have been branded "terrorists." While they may have cited the Law of Moses where it suited them, they were not actively teaching the Law of Moses to new recruits or supporting their fellow Jews in practicing it themselves.

The Sadducees

The Sadducees are the second most recognizable group in the New Testament. While the Sanhedrin was largely influenced by the Pharisees, the Temple was run primarily by those from the Sadducees. The reason was tied to their particular theological difference with the Pharisees.

Both the Pharisees and Sadducees represented the Jewish faith lived out in the public life. The major difference between the two groups was in their belief regarding resurrection. The Pharisees believed in a final resurrection from the dead, which would take place when the Messiah came to judge the world, while the Sadducees did not believe in this resurrection — or henceforth the Messiah or judgment day that logically follows.

I think this belief came about as a practical compromise under the Roman oppression. Rome, as a rule, did not tolerate religions with political aspirations, and certainly not religious groups who believed that the emperor would be deposed and judged along with their entire government and culture based on their loyalty and allegiance to a foreign God. Therefore, anyone who taught this way was not allowed to remain working in the Temple under Roman rule. Jewish priests could remain, however, by confessing a belief that this was the only life they had and, any judgment or consequences we faced, we would face in the present lifetime where those who had power and wealth could perhaps remain a bit above the consequences.

This was a practical compromise to keep Jewish priests in the Temple. To them, it made more sense to abandon the teaching of the Prophets, especially concerning the resurrection, and to focus instead on the ritual worship practices written in the Law of Moses. That was enough to appease the Roman government and keep the Temple from being taken over by Roman religious officials or completely destroyed.

The Sadducees believed that the Roman government and authority was tolerable. Over time, some of the individuals who enjoyed the power of important Temple officials kept those positions by keeping the Roman governors pleased, which meant they changed from merely being tolerant to being actively supportive of Roman rule. For them, though, the Law of Moses had to be made much more flexible, and, given the choice between the two, they would likely have sided with the Roman authority over the Law of Moses. After all, the Roman authority was very real and present to them, while God had not spoken to the Jewish people for nearly 500 years.

The Essenes

The last group was the Essenes. John the Baptist is probably the most famous of this group. They, like him, left the city life and lived lives of simplicity and devotion in the wilderness. They chose a steadfast devotion to the Law of Moses, motivated not by guilt or a desire to avoid breaking commandments, as did the Pharisees, but with a more prophetic focus that sought to ever be in God's presence. They, perhaps more than the other groups, recognized that, while the people had physically returned to Israel, spiritually they were still in exile. Instead of waging war physically, like the Zealots, they waged war spiritually through prayer and fasting. Rather than opposing or submitting to Roman rule publicly, they simply left the civilized world and started a new community in a place the Romans had no desire to control.

They abandoned the Roman authority in their lives and embraced the Law of Moses as their way of life. This made them outcasts to everyone outside their own group, free from the oppression of the Romans, but exempt from their protection as well. They called others away from their lives to repentance, a new start to a new community of faith, and they set the standards of sacrifice high — not as a price paid to get in, but as a necessity of freeing yourself from worldly things. They knew God was not of this world and they sought ways to seek Him out and join Him as best they were able.

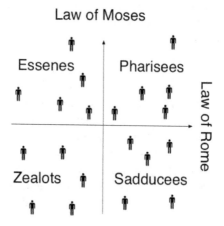

Chapter Three
The Pharisees and the Gospel of Matthew

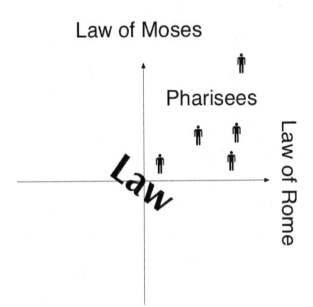

Law of Moses

Pharisees

Law

Law of Rome

Pharisees

The Pharisees come up as debate rivals of Jesus in the Gospels more than any other group of people and they are especially prominent in the Gospel of Matthew. It has been suggested that this rivalry was not because the Pharisees and Jesus were so different in their beliefs, but because they were so similar.[9] There is also evidence in the Gospels to support this. The list of the followers of Jesus contains Nicodemus, who is specifically noted as being a Pharisee,[10] possibly Joseph of Arimathea as well, and the most notable Pharisee in the

---

[9] Safrai, Shmuel. "Jesus and the Hasidim." *Jerusalem Perspective* 42-43-44. January-June (1994): 17. Web. August 4, 2016
[10] John 3:1

New Testament was Saul, who became Paul the Apostle.[11]

Both the disciples of Jesus and the Pharisees found themselves in conflict with Rome and both tried to focus more on obeying God as their primary authority. What was the difference between Jesus and the Pharisees then?

The Gospel of Matthew

Like Rabbi Hillel and Rabbi Shammai, the differences between the disciples of Jesus and the Pharisees came primarily from their interpretation of the Law of Moses. They adopted different methods of how to obey God's commandments and had different motivations of why to obey them. Ultimately, they saw the Law of Moses as having different purposes.

The Gospel of Matthew places a particular emphasis on the concept of God's Law and how it is lived out or "fulfilled" in our world. This was one of the major concerns of the Jews, and the Pharisees in particular. The Pharisees may have found their identity in their ability and willingness to keep the Law of Moses. Matthew's gospel provides the teachings of Jesus and the narrative of His ministry as a reinterpretation of that Law, showing the need for grace to be both received and given in order for the Law to be truly fulfilled.

Law of Moses

Purpose of the Law

One of the most important debates between Rabbi Hillel and Rabbi Shammai was on the subject of converting to Judaism. Hillel had traveled from outside of Israel to come and learn to be a Rabbi himself[12] and perhaps this personal challenge encouraged him to be very inclusive and accepting of those who wanted to convert to Judaism. Shammai, on the other hand, was much stricter regarding the upbringing, character, and commitment of those he took on as new converts.

---

[11] Philippians 3:5
[12] See http://www.jewishvirtuallibrary.org/jsource/biography/hillel.html

The Pharisees appear to have taken a little more influence from Rabbi Shammai in this regard, particularly in contrast with Jesus and his disciples. One of the complaints the Pharisees raised about Jesus and his disciples was that He spent time with "sinners" — tax collectors, prostitutes, and those of Gentile or mixed racial descent. They fully embraced the concept of being guilty by association, and while many respected Jesus and His teaching, they felt he was bringing down the Jewish name by associating with these people of questionable character and certainly should not have welcomed them in as disciples. They would have been thoroughly disgusted by the idea of the Gospel of Matthew being written by a former tax collector.

This issue of recruitment helps highlight the bigger purpose of the Law of Moses as a whole. In His Sermon on the Mount,[13] Jesus reinterprets the Law of Moses, beginning with a blessing and welcoming into God's kingdom of all the types of people you would not expect to be welcomed into anything. It is not the capable that are invited in, but those who are spiritually poor, hungry, meek, persecuted, and otherwise left out. Jesus first invites in those who have no chance of making it themselves. In the same chapter, He then goes on to teach that the Law of Moses is an all-or-nothing kind of law. We either fulfill all of it, or we break all of it. There is no competition for who can sin the least. Jesus appears both to lower the bar for entry into God's kingdom in one move and simultaneously raise the bar to stay there to an impossibly high level, which culminates in His command to love our enemies and to be *perfect* as our Heavenly Father is perfect.

The Pharisees, on the other hand, treated the Law of Moses like a filter. Those who kept the law were in, and those who did not were excluded. I think they criticized Jesus of guilt by association because it was one of the biggest fears they faced themselves. Unlike the Essenes, who got along quite nicely in the wilderness, associating only with other Essenes and devout Jews like themselves, the Pharisees had not quite given up hope on the rest of the world. They wanted to be agents of change in their world. They wanted to be in the world but not of the world,[14] but they feared they were failing,

---

13 Matthew 5-7
14 John 17

and that fear ate away and corrupted the very foundation of their faith. They were afraid to take in the spiritually poor, hungry, and those who had nothing to give, for fear of running out themselves. They were trying to use the Law of Moses to earn back God's trust and favor.

Matthew shows in the Sermon on the Mount that the purpose of the Law of Moses is to show us that none of us make it through the filter that the Pharisees try to make the law into and that it is only with God's help that any of us can find a way into God's kingdom. In fact, I think that Matthew's gospel could be read as a sort of narrative instruction book on making disciples, using the model that Jesus used. The account as a whole shows how Jesus, from His very birth, called forth followers from across the world — people who were not worthy in themselves (like the shepherds) and those who were foreigners (the Magi), and even his own young mother, who for all accounts looked like a woman pregnant out of wedlock. Jesus took all those people and made them followers and helped them to become proclaimers of His gospel to all the world. Indeed, Matthew's gospel ends with that very command — to take this gospel and make disciples of the entire world.

The political ramifications of this are simple, yet profound. *Everyone* is welcome. *Everyone* has to change. *No one* can make it without God's help. Matthew shows the first tells part one of that move is a movement from Israel as being God's chosen people to those who confess faith in Christ being God's chosen people. as Later, when Jesus sends His disciples out to Jerusalem, Judea, Samaria, and to the ends of the earth, and Luke (through his own gospel and Acts of the Apostles) will pick up where Matthew left off and finish the rest of that story through his own gospel and Acts of the Apostles.

Matthew does not have a less mature understanding of this move of God — he simply is writing to a different audience. It makes little sense to try to speak of God setting down roots in the seat of the Roman Empire when the Jews you are writing to (perhaps with Pharisee leanings) are not even sure if a gentile person can even become a Christian in the first place. Matthew's gospel meets those Pharisees right where they are and allows the story and work of Jesus to challenge and redirect their own zeal to follow God in their lives.

This concept of invitation and help for all is the first aspect of the Christian value of grace.

How to Follow the Law

Chapter 5 of Matthew addresses the purpose of the Law of Moses. Chapter 6 addresses *how* to follow that law; this chapter deals with some of the most practical and common forms of religious expression in the Jewish (or Christian) life. These expressions are giving, praying, fasting, and worrying.

Giving

I'm not sure that any of the four types of Jews in Jesus' time would have started off their list of religious habits with "giving to the needy." For that matter, I'm not sure that would go on the top of the list of religious practices for Christians today in our country, either. However, for Jesus, it does.

The Law of Moses contained dozens of laws and exceptions made specifically for the poor. While there is no expectation in either the Old or New Testament that poverty would ever be completely eradicated before Christ's return, God's people have always had a responsibility to use wealth, land, and resources to alleviate the effects of poverty around us. If you planted a field, you were commanded to leave the edges unharvested and set aside for the poor who had no fields themselves.[15] Alms were collected as offerings above and beyond the tithe that God asked to be set aside for Him and those who served in the Temple.[16] Even the sacrificial system itself had aspects of caring for the needs of those who did not have land and livestock.[17]

The Pharisees understood sacrifices and they understood tithing.[18] What they failed to understand was the spirit of generosity and gratitude that was to be nurtured by the opportunity to give. Jesus taught in Matthew 6:3-4 that giving should be done in secret and for

---

[15] Leviticus 19:9, 23:22
[16] Deuteronomy 15:11; Numbers 18:21-24
[17] Numbers 18:8-20
[18] Matthew 23:23

its own sake, not for the sake of reward or recognition. Jesus had a vision of the laws around sacrifices and giving that were reinforced, rather than contradicted by passages like Micah 6:6-8, which says:

6 "With what shall I come before the Lord,
   and bow myself before God on high?
Shall I come before him with burnt offerings,
   with calves a year old?
7 Will the Lord be pleased with[a] thousands of rams,
   with ten thousands of rivers of oil?
Shall I give my firstborn for my transgression,
   the fruit of my body for the sin of my soul?"
8 He has told you, O man, what is good;
   and what does the Lord require of you
but to do justice, and to love kindness,
   and to walk humbly with your God?[19]

What Micah taught and Jesus reemphasized in Matthew 6 was that the opportunity to bring sacrifices, to tithe for the service of the Temple and to give beyond that allowed the Jews to do justice, love kindness, and walk humbly with their God. In order to nurture that character in them, they needed to let go of their wealth and resources and allow God to use it to reshape and remake them. It was, and is, a matter of giving up control of our possessions and ultimately ourselves so that we are free to practice being God's people.

The political values of Jesus include the value of generosity. This generosity is not measured by effectiveness or efficiency of managing poverty. Jesus taught that we should give so that our left hand does not know what our right hand is doing. It is a generosity of giving for the sake of the giver, not just the recipient. We cannot understand the value of grace without the value of generosity.

Praying

Prayer is the next item on Jesus' list of how to follow God's Law. Prayer was something the Pharisees would have had plenty of experience doing. It was customary for disciples of Jewish rabbis to ask their teacher how to pray. These prayers would be handed down

---

[19] Micah 6:6-8, ESV

through the generations then in some powerful ways. Think, for example, of the power of Psalm 23, a prayer of David, who lived 1000 years before Christ and whose words are still recited by many Jews and Christians all over the world today!

Prayer itself, and particularly passing along prayers to students, is a powerful act. The prayers we pray over and over again become a picture of the invisible God we worship. Others actually "see" God in our prayers. If you take just a few minutes to read through a few more of the Psalms, you will quickly see what I mean. They are filled with imagery that depicts God as warrior, king, shepherd, healer, bringer of justice, and bringer of mercy. To pass on a prayer is another way of saying, "This is how I see God."

The Pharisees had many prayers and many were long and elaborate.[20] This may have been done in attempt to create something worthy of a God they saw as majestic and set apart from them. Curiously, Jesus compares this same concept of prayer as something the "hypocrites" (or actors) and the Gentiles do. I can think of few insults that would sting a Pharisee as much as having their prayers compared to pretenders and pagans. Yet, for all their efforts in creating the perfect prayers, they really had no more effect than the others and left those who heard them praying with a distorted view of God.

Jesus had a different idea about how to pray. He started His prayer off by naming God "Our Father in Heaven." He addressed God in a way that portrayed more intimacy than the Jews had dared to attempt. As God's legitimate son, Jesus of course could address God like that, but — incredibly — He shared that privilege with His disciples when He taught them to pray like this.

The next line, "hallowed be your name," raises the reverence and thereby puts even more emphasis on that intimacy. This is not a prayer to a God we do not know. It is a prayer to a God we know well. The portrait of God that Jesus introduces in this prayer is not a God made more common than the prayers of the Pharisees. It is a portrait that is more holy and majestic and powerful because this God can hold the entire world in His hand and get down in the dirt on His hands and knees to look you in the eye, face to face, all at the

---

[20] Luke 18:11

same time.

The prayer is short and this initial address to God is followed by four requests and a footnote for the disciples. The first request is for God's kingdom to intervene and conquer this world so that God may rule on earth as He does in Heaven. This first request is an incredibly political one and echoes the prayers of all the Jewish people (with the possible exception of some Sadducees) that God would send the Messiah to deliver them from the rule of Rome. This is the kind of prayer that is behind every Christian who prays for a Christian president to be elected. Jesus does not pick out a single enemy in this prayer. He leaves it open to invite God to come and conquer all of them, including ourselves. This is significant because sometimes I am my own worst enemy when it comes to keeping me from following God's will.

The next request is for our "daily bread." Here he addresses the confusion that I sometimes have distinguishing between wants and needs, distinguishing from my preferences and God's will. The phrase "daily bread" reflects back to the 40 years in the wilderness that the Hebrew people experienced under Moses' leadership.[21] This, too, is a political statement, as it challenges the current factions of leadership to move back toward a time when God Himself led the people and fed them each day Himself. This is the opposite of picking yourself up by your bootstraps. This is putting your own desires aside and recognizing that your needs — your most basic needs — can only be met by God's providence. This is not the politics of communism or democracy. This is the economy of a welfare nation where everyone is on welfare and God is the one footing the bill. That may seem a bit extreme, but is that so far from the truth even today? Where does our wealth come from? Where does our food come from? Do we create the land on which to grow food? What keeps that land in our own possession? Do we cause it to rain so that crops might grow? We rely on God far more than we often realize until tragedies and ecological catastrophes cause our agriculture and economies to fail and we realize we succeeded only because of God's blessing the whole time. No matter who we are or where we are — it is God who ultimately supplies our daily bread.

---

[21] Exodus 16

This welfare concept leads right into the next request of God — to forgive our debts. Luke records that we are to ask forgiveness of "sins" (ἁμαρτίας) while Matthew uses the word "debts" (ὀφειλήματα). To ask forgiveness of debts is to admit inability or unwillingness to pay what you owe. I believe that here in Matthew, Jesus teaches that much of what we need forgiveness for are not intentional acts of defiance against God, but instead our inability and unwillingness to give Him what He is due. So what is due Him? In light of His provision for us in the previous request, we owe Him gratitude at the very least. If we take time to consider how much God provides for us and our well-being, the only way we could pay Him back might possibly be using everything He has given us for His benefit — or, to put it another way, living our entire lives in worship and service to God. Since we do not do that, either by inability or unwillingness, our ledger with God drops further and further into the red each day. We owe God more worship and service than we can repay, and yet we still choose to take what He gives for granted and live our own way each day. So Jesus teaches us that we can and we should ask forgiveness of that debt whenever we pray.

This request has a qualifier attached to it. Not only should we seek forgiveness of our own debt to God, but we should then take on his character of generosity and treat others who have debts with us the same way God treats us. This hearkens back to His teaching on the Law when Jesus tells us to "be perfect as your Heavenly Father is perfect" and to do so by loving your enemies and not just your friends.[22] Jesus calls us into an impossible economy, at least by human standards, precisely because it does not rely on human strength, only human participation. The foundation of this economy that Jesus sets up is that God will provide, and we must be grateful and generous.

The last request of this prayer is, in the light of this impossible political/economic relationship we are requesting God to accept us into, do not let us be led into temptation. As Jesus points out later on in Matthew, it is not money that is temptation or evil, it is the love of money. That is only a small part of the temptation they faced, though. They faced persecution and fear for their lives and the lives

---

[22] Matthew 5:43-48

of their families. They faced temptation to use their new influence and connection to Jesus to manipulate and extort others. They could have charged money for their preaching, teaching, and healing. They could have demanded loyalty and tribute. They could have asked for political power — and we face all those same temptations today as well. Lord, do not lead us into those places of temptation... and when we wander into them, please deliver us from that evil that is so quick to consume and become us.

The footnote that Matthew has regarding prayer is a repetition of the prayer for forgiveness. Jesus makes it clear that this relationship with God is not one-sided. It requires our participation. Whatever debts we are willing to forgive others will be forgiven us, but whatever debts we hold on to will be held against us as well. In the politics of God's kingdom, we are not allowed to wield oppressive power over one another because, in relation to God, every one of us is living on God's grace. God will not allow that grace to be used as a prop to put us above one another. The prayer Jesus teaches shows a grace that puts everyone on equal footing, in right relationship with God and each other.

Fasting

Fasting is the last of the three positive religious practices taught in the Sermon on the Mount. Like giving and prayer, Jesus teaches that it should be done in secret and not to gain the sympathy or admiration of others. This requires a bit more forethought with fasting, though. Both prayer and giving are more or less instantaneous activities that require a specific effort to do. While prayer can last for hours, each moment requires intentional effort.

Fasting, on the other hand, is more of a lack of activity instead of an instantaneous act. Fasting always takes time and has unintentional effects on us. The longer we fast, the more tired and irritable we become, and eventually even our physical appearance changes. It becomes noticeable to those who see us, often before we see it ourselves. So Jesus taught that we need to make preparations to make ourselves look normal if we are to keep the practice hidden from the public view.

What are the political ramifications of fasting? The act of fasting in the Jewish and Christian tradition is not just and absence of eating. It is a trade-off of sorts, where the people choose to dedicate the time and effort and resources normally spent on taking care of their own legitimate needs to spend in gratitude to God and often seeking after spiritual guidance or needs as well. It is a small attempt, if you will, to stop the constant indebtedness we have to God and to make some kind of payment back. It shows allegiance to God's authority by putting God first in our life priorities instead of somewhere down below ourselves and our own needs.

What did the Pharisees think about this? I think they would have believed this wholeheartedly. Fasting was one of their ways of trying to get God's attention and win His favor. Perhaps they recalled the story of Jonah where an entire city of wicked people was spared because they all fasted and sought forgiveness. I imagine there were many Pharisees trying to reenact that story in the city of Jerusalem in the first century.

Yet here again, Jesus specifically tells them they are to do it in secret. You cannot make a very loud noise, and certainly not a loud enough noise to reach Heaven if everyone is fasting and praying in secret, behind their own closed doors. He is reflecting back to the beginning of this His prayer though and this picture He paints of a "Heavenly Father" who is close enough to hear our whispers and mighty enough that no amount of religious fervor and fanaticism has a hope of bending His will to do what we want Him to do. We cannot manipulate God — not as individuals, and not as an entire world seeking Him. This is not because He is so distant, for that could possibly be overcome by reaching and seeking. It is because He is so good and loving and any request we make outside His will would be less loving and less good for us than what He intends to do anyway.

Fasting does not bend God's will to ours. It bends our will to God's. The value of grace that Jesus teaches, as in the practices of prayer and giving, is one that is not controlling or manipulative. Grace is given in the trust that God will lead and provide for us.

Worrying

The final note on religious practices that Jesus teaches on in His Sermon on the Mount is the practice of worrying. You may not have considered this a religious practice before because it does not necessarily seem religious or something you have to practice. For many of us, worrying just comes naturally. However, there are certainly times where anxiety takes over our lives, encouraging us to worry with religious zeal, and with practice, we do learn how to worry better. We learn what kind of medications we can take to allow us to worry longer without as many immediate detrimental health effects. We find activities to immerse ourselves in to distract ourselves from the source of our anxieties. Indeed, there are entire social groups that form around the concept of worry.

That is where this all becomes political. If the Pharisees lived in our culture, they would have official t-shirts made that would say, "Exile: Been there, done that, got the t-shirt. Never want to go back." All that they believed and did was rooted in the constant worry that God was going to completely abandon them. So they went out of their way to make sure they did not do anything that even approached breaking the commandments, and encouraged everyone around them to do the same as much as possible.

Jesus again pointed back to the picture of the Heavenly Father who loves and provides for all His children, and the futility of worrying. The faith of the Pharisees, the very faith they were trying to foster all around, was being squelched by their own fear. Instead of letting go of the fear and embracing faith, they spread their fear and anxiety in the name of a faith they could not hold themselves. Well-intentioned preaching and teaching became manipulative fear tactics, extorting the goodwill and trust of those around them.

That same fear is rampant in our culture today. The media and politicians know that spreading fear is the fastest and cheapest way to be heard and to gather a sympathetic crowd. How many times was the world supposed to end in the last decade? How often do we hear the worst-case scenario of rumors and strategies of escape or self-defense before finding out the facts of a situation? How much of the courage of our culture and the American sense of adventure have been lost due to overprotective parents and fears about every possible harm that might potentially come our way? Scrolling through social media, I am struck not only by the amount of negative news covered, but especially how much of it is intended to inspire fear or anxiety to move me to buy something or do something to protect myself.

Real living faith in Christ leaves no room for that fear or worry. We are not to be caught up in that fear ourselves and we certainly are not to be spreading it. That fear denies God's powerful authority and loving kindness toward us and the rest of the world. If we are to practice faith and the value of grace, we must abandon all politics of fear.

Why to obey

While chapters 5 and 6 of Matthew show the purpose of the Law of Moses and some practical ways of actually following that law, the Sermon on the Mount concludes with the explanation of *why* to follow God's law. Jesus transitions to the conclusion of His sermon, moving from the practice of worrying to the attitude (and often practice) of judging others. If worrying is the active form of fear and doubt, judging is the passive-aggressive form. The purpose of judging is, more often than not, self-justification. If I don't feel good about my life, I try to find others who I think are worse than myself in order to make myself feel better.

That is exactly what the Pharisees did to those who did not follow them. One of the best examples comes from the parable of the Pharisee and the tax collector.[23] I have often wondered why this particular parable did not make it into Matthew's gospel. Perhaps, being a former tax collector himself, he felt it would have been a bit too pointed and self-congratulating. Maybe he chose not to share that story in his gospel in order to take the humble attitude of the tax collector at prayer rather than the self-righteous Pharisee.

---

[23] See Luke 18:9-14. (I have often wondered why this particular parable did not make it into Matthew's gospel. Perhaps, being a former tax collector himself, he felt it would have been a bit too pointed and self-congratulating. Maybe he chose not to share that story in his gospel in order to take the humble attitude of the tax collector at prayer rather than the self-righteous Pharisee.)

Jesus contrasts a Pharisee and a tax collector at prayer. The Pharisee, who would be considered an upstanding citizen, stands in the Temple and thanks God that he is not like the wicked tax collector and then tells God what spiritual deeds he has done. The tax collector, refuses to even raise his head, but humbly begs forgiveness. Jesus says that it is the tax collector, not the Pharisee who goes home justified that day.

In a dog-eat-dog world, the only way up is by stepping on the heads of those beneath you. This kind of world is a corruption of the gift that God has given us in creation and it is not the politics of His Kingdom. Our exploitation of one another is always marked by judging each other and we will always find fear sitting at the bottom of it all.

Matthew 7:6 is a curious verse that almost seems out of place in this lesson about judging. Jesus says:

> *"Do not give dogs what is holy, and do not cast your pearls before pigs, lest they trample them underfoot and turn to attack you."*

At first glance, this looks like a suggestion to go right back to judging one another. However, a closer reading of the previous example of taking the log out of your own eye before you start to pick at specks in the lives of those around you shows something else in this teaching. This lesson about judging is not only about the passive-aggressive form of self-justification and feeling superior to others. Jesus is pointing out here that our own efforts to fix or "help" others are often just another form of judging others as well. I feel good about myself when I "help" someone worse off than me and am able to bring them to a better state of being. It is this Savior complex that we sometimes fall into that is a whitewashed version of self-justification, trying to deceive everyone, even ourselves... especially ourselves into believing that we are something we are not. In the politics of God's kingdom, there is only one Savior (John 14:6), and we all stand equally in need of rescuing. Those who try to take the place of Jesus in saving others will find their efforts unable, unwanted, and, as Jesus points out, they will often find themselves at the bottom of the heap, at the mercy of the very people they judged in need of their efforts.

In direct contrast to the politics of fear and judgment, Jesus introduces a politics of generosity and gratitude. Here again, Jesus shows His portrait of God as "Our Father in Heaven" who knows how and delights in giving good gifts to His children. Jesus points out that if we, as imperfect people, know how to love our children, how much more so does our Father in Heaven. We cannot base our political agendas on our own strength, as the Pharisees did. It must be founded on a trust in God's provision for us and gratitude for that gift.

Jesus then turns the table on our relationships with each other. Instead of "an eye for an eye", the command is to treat one another, not according to their works, but according to our own preferences for ourselves. Whatever I want in life I should give to others. Whatever I think is fair for me, I should make sure my neighbor has. This is not a policy of fairness and equality — this is a policy of generosity. Taken literally, this does not mean that I will receive everything I want. It means I would receive what everyone else around me wants, and I would give them what I want. It is not mechanical and cold, it is messy and awkward — so why would Jesus tell us this and claim that this is the culmination of the Law of Moses and the Prophets of God?

You can program a machine to calculate cold fairness, but when you give a command like this "Golden Rule," to treat others as you wish to be treated, it forces you to live in community and interact with one another and it puts you in position to truly love and get to know one another. Real love, true healthy relationships, treat each other not as objects to be acted upon, but as subjects to learn and interact with. They are relationships that are not stagnant, but grow and change over time. This is the politics of God's Kingdom: that we should be interconnected in ever-growing, ever-changing relationships with one another as we learn and love together.

This is the only kind of politics that is inclusive enough to invite people in. The politics of judgment draws lines in the sand and forbids change in either party. The politics of God continually invites that change in everyone on the scene. It is easier to judge and there are a multitude of factors we can use to divide ourselves from each other (the wide path), but it is difficult to remain humble enough and fearlessly faithful enough to trust in God's provision and seek to love others we do not yet know how to love. So we simply start by loving them the way we would like to be loved ourselves.

The conclusion of the sermon teaches of God's judgment upon all of us with three brief illustrations. The first is the comparison of false prophets (or leaders) who, like those with Savior complexes, come with good tidings and intents to "help," while inwardly they are only trying to set themselves above the crowd. Good trees and bad trees are judged by their fruit. Fruit, throughout scripture, often refers not only to the actions of individuals, but the multiplication of communities through the loving relationships between their people. Fear-mongering and judgment may draw a crowd for a time and spread like a fire, but that kind of community does not grow organically. It burns itself out, often turning inward like those dogs and pigs Jesus warned about. Only the messy work of invitation to transforming relationships based in the faith and security of and gratitude for God's provision have the means of becoming a community that bears "good fruit."

To further emphasize that point, Jesus gives a second example of those who try to bear fruit on their own strength. They may build communities around themselves and may do good works of great value, but they will not enter God's kingdom. God's kingdom is not entered into by passing a test, being a certain kind of person, or any other form of earning your way in. God's kingdom is not a status — it is a relationship with God Himself in Jesus Christ. The Pharisees who worked so hard to earn that relationship could never have it because, in keeping God at a distance for those who did not deserve Him, they kept God at a distance from themselves as well, in an infinite distance of always being aware He is there but never being good enough to approach Him. Jesus teaches plainly that this is not what the Law of Moses teaches, nor is it an accurate picture of our Heavenly Father.

This is politics of good news, not bad news. God is here with us. From the beginning of Matthew's gospel when the angels approach Mary and Joseph and tell them "do not be afraid," they brought tidings of great joy and peace and hope for our world. It is not news we can simply sit back and enjoy, though. It is an invitation to live in the world, with the law of man, yet finding our strength to transform the very world around us with our support from God Himself as taught through His Law. God's Law guides us into cultivating the character of God's people, and God Himself gives us the strength and ability to live and be part of God's new creation of a transformed world, brought under the rule of our Father in Heaven. This is the political value of grace.

The Rest of the Story

The following 21 chapters of Matthew take those very concepts that Jesus preached about in the Sermon on the Mount and show how He lived out those teachings and taught them to His disciples. The Sermon is the theory and illustrations; the rest of this gospel is filled with the practical examples and reiterations of God's Law. It is much like the Law of Moses itself. One can read the Decalogue,[24] or the Ten Commandments, and get a pretty good idea of how to live according to God's will. The rest of the five books of Moses are filled with practical examples of how to (and often how not to) follow that law.

Both the Law of Moses and the Gospel of Matthew contain a decisive moment of God's salvation and a commission. Exodus tells the story of God calling the Hebrew people out of slavery in Egypt and making them His people. Matthew tells the story of Christ's death on the cross for our sins and resurrection that called us out of slavery to sin and invited us into an eternal kingdom. It was the love of God in Jesus Christ, following that command to do to others whatever you wish them to do for you, that led Jesus to the cross to die for our sin. Moses commissioned the Israelites then to go and live for God in the Promised Land at the end of Deuteronomy. Jesus, at the end of Matthew, tells us to go into the entire world, following God's Spirit that conquers the world with grace, by inviting all people into a transforming relationship with Him and His people.

The Law for Today

One of the main motivations behind the Pharisee movement was

---

[24] Exodus 20:1-17

comparison. If they looked better than others, particularly in the eyes of God, they believed God would treat them better. While it is true that they sometimes compared themselves with other Jewish believers, there was always a world full of Gentiles that they believed they stood head and shoulders above just by being born a Jew. This prejudice of comparison may seem like a polite way of handling the stress and challenges that they faced in their world, but it is the seedbed of racism, classism, and every other prejudice that plagues our world.

Does that mean that comparing is wrong in itself? No, it simply means that varying degrees of wrong are still wrong, no matter what kind of excuses we bring up. When it is done with the motivation of trying to make yourself seem right without any actual change of behavior on your part, it is simply prejudice.

It is not just individuals who do this, either. Entire communities — entire nations — have been guilty of using comparison to justify their own actions. In the 1930s, some people in an economically broken and war-torn Germany chose to take out their frustrations on the Jews — not because the Jews had started World War I or had brought the country down so low, but because they were viewed as foreigners who were not loyal to the German nation. They were portrayed first as malicious and conniving villains, and eventually as something less than human. A nation had lost their way and felt as if they had lost God's favor and they sought to win it back by showing they were better than the Jews.

These are usually not planned movements. They are simply sins that are tolerated and that grow over time. They grow because while I may delude myself into believing I truly am better than the people I judge — the reality of life every day proves to me otherwise. Inside, I will always be my own harshest critic because no one but God knows the depths of my sin the way I do. I feel guilty, and that guilt grows and continues to gnaw within me until finding new and bigger ways to judge others becomes a coping skill to try to soothe the guilt that grows within me. Soon everything is excusable, save for one thing: asking forgiveness. That is the one thing a Pharisee could not do.

Asking forgiveness admits wrongdoing and fault, which may exclude you from the ranks of religious leaders forever. The Pharisees believed it removed you from God's favor. Some people act as though admitting you are wrong, even once, completely cancels out any good you have ever done. This applies to communities as well as individuals. Businesses cannot apologize without losing business. Nations cannot apologize without looking weak. We unintentionally teach that only the weak apologize — demanding it only of children (sometimes) and of criminals. We have plenty of laws to measure each other by, but little concept or energy directed toward grace — the aspect that actually makes us better.

Jesus never casts out the Law. He simply reintroduced grace. In all his words and deeds, Jesus showed that to truly live as God's people, we need both law and grace. Grace is our entry into God's kingdom. It gives us accessibility and opportunity that we do not deserve. However, it is law that allows us to stay in those places. Left to our own devices we have no knowledge of how to grow and improve, and often very little motivation to do so. This becomes even more prevalent in our relationships with others... especially those who have different desires than ourselves. For those who have experienced grace, it becomes a law as to how they are to treat others. Law and grace go hand in hand.

Where is the grace in our politics? We have plenty of law and we and bring more into it every day, whether it is interpretations of human law or God's law... but where do we find political grace?

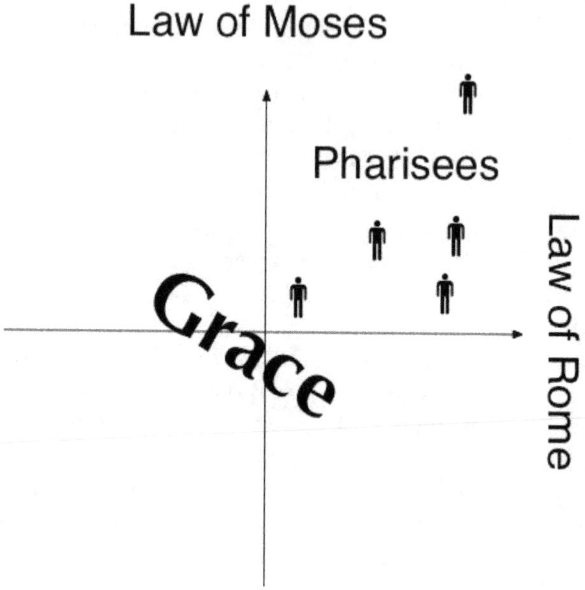
Law of Moses
Pharisees
Law of Rome
Grace

Chapter Four

The Zealots and the Gospel of Mark

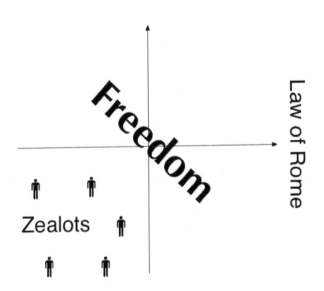

Zealots

In any stressful situations, our brains naturally release adrenaline that readies our muscles for action and prepares us for one of two actions: fight or flight. Under the stress of Roman occupation, the Zealots chose to fight.

There is considerable debate over whether the Zealots existed during the time of Jesus or if they only emerged just prior to the fall of Jerusalem in AD 70. Johnson and Lookadoo point out that the name of Simon the Zealot suggests that the title may have existed during the time when Luke–Acts was written, as Luke distinguishes him from Simon Peter (Luke 6:15). He is described using a different word, "Cananaean", in Mark 3:18. If one takes the name "Simon the Zealot" as a reference to the same group Josephus mentions, the Zealots must have been a recognizable political group much earlier than Josephus allows. Three others appear in the crucifixion story who seem more likely to have been involved in Zealot-like activity. The first of these is Barabbas, who "committed murder in the insurrection" (Mark 15:7). This "insurrection" may have been related to an early Jewish freedom movement. The two people between whom Jesus is crucified are also described as "bandits," a term that Josephus uses to describe elements of the resistance movement that may not have been directly related to the Zealots but were nevertheless involved in the Jewish fight for freedom (Mark 15:27).[25]

The issue for us is not whether or not the Zealots were a full-fledged, official political group. The issue is what kinds of people held religious and political beliefs that were sympathetic with the ones that came about when the Zealots did emerge as an official group. Indeed, we will see that there may have been some collusion between different political groups during the crucifixion that came about in response to the new political scene Jesus was creating in Galilee and Jerusalem. For those Jews who chose to fight occupation, who was considered an enemy and how did those Jews fight against them?

The Gospel of Mark

The Gospel of Mark is an action-packed gospel. It is the shortest of the three gospels and focuses less on the teachings of Jesus (as opposed to Matthew's gospel) and more on the deeds of Jesus. The common sequence that occurs over and over again in Matthew is Jesus went to... (somewhere) and did... (something) and *immediately* (something happened). Much of Mark's gospel could be written just copying that sentence and filling in the blanks with new words. It is a gospel that shows the Son of Man on a mission and nothing will stop him until He gets there.

---

[25] Johnson, B. T., & Lookadoo, J. (2012, 2013, 2014, 2015). Zealot. In J. D. Barry, D. Bomar, D. R. Brown, R. Klippenstein, D. Mangum, C. Sinclair Wolcott, ... W. Widder (Eds.), *The Lexham Bible Dictionary*. Bellingham, WA: Lexham Press.

It is the story of a conquering king who could say with Julius Caesar after his short and decisive victory at Zela, "*veni vidi vici*" ("I came, I saw, I conquered").[26] While early Christians may not have been familiar with this work, they likely had heard stories of Julius Caesar and were familiar with the Roman concept of a conquering king. We know there was much excitement surrounding this idea because the crowds around Jesus gathered larger and larger as He approached Jerusalem. Mark 11 shows a people seeking a change in political regime, and not just any change. They wanted to be ruled by a Jewish king: one from the lineage of David, and one who would not allow the imposition of the Roman Empire.

Who is the enemy?

The Zealots' Enemies

Public enemies

Rome had learned the art of political persuasion in running an empire. They allowed their colonized countries to retain indigenous leaders, so long as those leaders pledged their complete loyalty to Rome. It allowed for the appearance of self-rule, while actually making puppet leaders out of conquered kings. If the Herodians were any example of typical puppet kings, they did less to maintain cultural identity and more to transition in Roman culture into these territories. These puppet leaders, the Herodians, would have been among the chief enemies of the Zealots — those who betrayed their own people.

A very close second would have been the Romans themselves. The primary threats were the governor and the Roman soldiers stationed in their cities, although travelers and merchants were probably not exempt. The "zeal" for which the Zealots were named may have been claimed as a zeal for God's Law,[27] similar in concept to the

---

[26] Suetonius, Lives of the Twelve Caesars:Julius from penelope.uchicago.edu

[27] "Hengel characterizes this movement as one that demanded a total separation from Hellenistic encroachments. It emphasized the purity of the temple, a rigorous and precise understanding of the law, a readiness to fight enemies both external and internal to Judaism, and a willingness to sacrifice one's life for the cause. Phinehas and Elijah were historic exemplars for the movement, and Hengel traces continuity from the earlier Maccabean revolt through the more radical elements of first century bc Pharisaism." Johnson, B. T., & Lookadoo, J. (2012,

Pharisees, but they focused almost exclusively on the traditions prohibiting Jews from associating with Gentiles.[28] Perhaps they believed that the rest of the law could not be followed while they were continually in the presence of Gentiles. The mixture of racial and religious purity they sought to facilitate, particularly in Jerusalem, was probably derived from a complex series of factors — many stemming from the same fear and frustration that also plagued the Pharisees and fueled their legalism.

What surprises me about both groups is not the way the groups dug deep into the Law of Moses to bring some support in dealing with the Roman rule. It is the excuses they made when their official acts contradicted both Roman rule and the Law of Moses. For instance, the Pharisees created a loophole in caring for others by claiming the money they would have given, they gave to the Temple instead.[29] In a further extreme, the Zealots apparently found murder, which is forbidden by the sixth commandment, to be an acceptable act when it was done to Roman authorities.

Perspective of the Problem

The Zealots saw all the suffering the Jews experienced as *a political problem with spiritual effects*. The poverty, the sickness, all of the ills they faced, they traced back to being a consequence of Roman occupation. This had the effect of broadening their potential enemies from the Roman governor and guards to all Romans, to all Roman sympathizers, and eventually to anyone who had the possibility of being a Roman sympathizer. It is this kind of paranoia that grows into a mindset that says you are either with me or against me, either friend or foe — there are no innocent bystanders in my war I'm fighting.

2013, 2014, 2015). "Zealot." In J. D. Barry, D. Bomar, D. R. Brown, R. Klippenstein, D. Mangum, C. Sinclair Wolcott, ... W. Widder (Eds.), *The Lexham Bible Dictionary*. Bellingham, WA: Lexham Press.

[28] "While no specific law forbade interaction with a Gentile, the purity laws in the OT often forced a Jew to limit interaction with Gentiles. Jewish traditions built on the law forbade interaction. Peter's statement goes against this entire system." Barry, J. D., Heiser, M. S., Custis, M., Mangum, D., & Whitehead, M. M. (2012). *Faithlife Study Bible* (Ac 10:28). Bellingham, WA: Logos Bible Software.

[29] Mark 7:11

Mark's gospel shows us how Jesus completely turns the table on the mindset of the Zealots, proving the problem to be *a spiritual problem with political ramifications*. He shows that the spiritual forces are the source of the suffering the Jews face, and it is that suffering that creates further conflict with the Gentiles and the Romans in particular. Jesus begins by redefining the enemies of the Jews and ends by showing them a new way to fight for their own freedom and the return of the Rule of God on earth.

The Enemies of Jesus

Evil Spirits

Mark's gospel skips the birth narrative and the first 30 years of Jesus' life, choosing instead to focus on the 3 years of His ministry and journey to the cross in Jerusalem. Unlike Moses in the Old Testament, who has a special birth narrative (as Matthew compares to Jesus in his gospel account), Mark writes the story of Jesus more like the stories of the Judges of Israel who were "raised up" by God during Israel's time of need, delivered them, and then disappeared into the depths of history.

Mark begins with a scripture reference from the prophet Isaiah and identifies John the Baptist as the fulfillment of this prophecy. John has his own role to play in this narrative, but he never overshadows Jesus and never steps into the role as conqueror himself. He is a witness, "a voice crying in the wilderness," just as Isaiah described. He provides the introduction to this action-packed drama, points out Jesus as the main character by baptizing Him, and then quickly steps aside. Even though Jesus has a powerful introduction onto the scene, His transition from anonymity to celebrity status is anything but easy.

Mark says, *immediately* after being baptized, Jesus was led by the Spirit of God into the wilderness where He was "being tempted by Satan." No time to pack a bag or get prepared — no, the first enemy that Jesus is to face in this work is the greatest evil of all, Satan himself. From the very first chapter, Mark makes it clear to us that this is a spiritual war that Jesus is waging on our behalf and that everything else flows out of this. Nor is this a quick battle. It says Jesus is out in the wilderness for 40 days, fasting and praying, while being tempted and being ministered to by the angels. Luke provides a longer account of this, but Mark focuses on the point that Jesus went into battle the first day on the job.

Upon his return from the wilderness, and after John was arrested, Jesus began preaching this message:

> *"The time is fulfilled, and the kingdom of God is at hand; repent and believe in the gospel.[30]"*

This is the announcement. This is what the Jews had been waiting for. This is the gospel.

Every king needs an army, so Jesus next goes on to recruit an army for this movement. He begins with four fishermen who would become some of his most famous followers: Two sets of brothers Simon (Peter) and Andrew, as well as James and John, the sons of Zebedee. Jesus calls them out of their boats and *immediately* they drop everything and follow Him. He takes them into the city of Capernaum, wasting no time. He heads straight for the synagogue and begins preaching there and *immediately* (are you catching a theme here?) there was a man with an unclean spirit that cried out,

"What have you to do with us, Jesus of Nazareth? Have you come to destroy us? I know who you are — the Holy One of God.[31]

Jesus did not even have a chance to get a bath from his 40 days in the wilderness fighting Satan, and already He was being called out by evil spirits in the synagogue. This incident reveals two things about the spiritual state of Israel.

1. The evil spirits were very aware of the presence of Jesus, even before He had a large crowd following Him. Perhaps they heard about his showdown in the wilderness. Maybe they were just keenly aware of the presence of God among them. Either way, they were

---

[30] *The Holy Bible: English Standard Version.* (2001). (Mk 1:15). Wheaton: Standard Bible Society.
[31] The Holy Bible: English Standard Version. (2001). (Mk 1:24). Wheaton: Standard Bible Society."

aware, and they were worried.

2. The presence of evil spirits was not limited to Gentile places or even just common public areas. Apparently, it was not difficult for them to infiltrate Jewish sacred areas, such as the synagogue here. The way it is written, I am unsure whether this possessed man entered into the synagogue after Jesus, or if the presence and teaching of Jesus actually brought this evil spirit to the forefront of one of the regular attendees of this synagogue. Either way, Mark gives us a clear description of the depth of spiritual distress this place was in, the inability of the Jewish people to rid themselves of these evil spirits, and the swift and powerful deliverance that Jesus provides these people and their hometown religious center. With only a few words, the evil spirit is violently torn from the person and the people are left astounded.

Mark points out that it is not just a new teaching or interpretation that inspires them. It is the authority that Jesus wields — even over evil spirits themselves. It is His power to do what they cannot do themselves. Mark also presents us with the challenge of acknowledging the very real power that spiritual forces have in our lives, for good or evil, and the political priority in addressing spiritual issues.

Disease

The second enemy that Jesus faced was disease. C. Byrley writes,

> Sickness and disability are the physical manifestations of the presence of suffering in the world, connected to the weakness and frailty of the human body due to the effects of sin. Certain sicknesses or disabilities were tied to ritual impurity and could exclude a person from public worship in Israel. As a sign of his restoration of all things, Jesus' public ministry was marked by frequent healing of the sick and disabled.[32]

---

[32] Byrley, C. (2014). "Sickness and Disability." D. Mangum, D. R. Brown, R. Klippenstein, & R. Hurst (Eds.), Lexham Theological Wordbook. Bellingham, WA: Lexham Press.

As soon as Jesus left the synagogue, he was met with sickness and disease. First, Peter takes him to visit his mother-in-law who is stricken with a fever. "Seizing her hand,[33]" Jesus raised her up and she was immediately healed of the fever and began serving them all. It is easy to miss the importance of the short time line between these events, particularly if we come from a more science-oriented culture. Consider this in a contemporary first-world context. If you mother-in-law was sick in the hospital, you might bring your newfound friend, the Messiah, to visit her if you believed He had the power to heal. But after simply reaching out and raising her up from the bed, would you have her cook dinner for you and Jesus? Or would you rather wait until you were sure the illness had passed and she was no longer contagious?

Nothing seemed to stop him. I think the four disciples may have caught that idea in the synagogue when Jesus cast out the evil spirit, but after this healing done with only a touch, they were sure of it. So was everyone else. Mark 1 ends with a description of the whole town bringing their sick out to Jesus to be healed. In a day without antibiotics and safe, sterile hospitals to perform surgery, most medical aid was limited to herbal remedies and chicken soup... if you could afford them. Serious injury or illness among the poor was often a death sentence. Jesus was not just fighting a fever here, a lame foot there — He took on the crippling power of illness and injury itself over the community of God's people.

Those with more than a passing knowledge of Jesus will not be surprised by the many stories of Jesus' healing in all four the gospels. Mark however appears to set sickness and disease up as one of the three common enemies the Jews faced and that Jesus routinely claimed victory over... and not just simple victory, but extravagant and powerful victory. There are no rituals performed or sacrifices made on behalf of these victims. Jesus simply conquers with a word or a touch.

The word that Mark reports on the lips of all those who watched Jesus do these things was: Authority. Jesus uses his authority to bring

---

[33] Guelich, R. A. (1998). *Mark 1–8:26* (Vol. 34A, p. 62). Dallas: Word, Incorporated.

healing and restoration to the victims of suffering wherever he met them. He did not seek them out, or create the pretense the His sole purpose was to bring healing, but He did not shy away from the crowd of those who came to Him seeking to be made whole. Jesus showed that life was sacred and demonstrated that bringing physical healing was a way to reverse the effects of sin and suffering in His kingdom.

People with Authority

Authority was the very thing the Zealots wanted. They were likely unaware of the depths of the spiritual bondage they were in and they were unable to fight the effects of it in illness and disease. So they chose to take it out on the Romans, who they believed were the source of all this suffering. The agenda was politically driven, and this was not wrong. There were political issues that needed to be addressed. It was not holistic, though. There was no plan of how to address those who would be hurt by the detachment from the Roman Empire (which included many merchants who enjoyed the freedom to travel in part because of the Romans) and the agenda did not make provisions to care for those caught in the crossfire of the inevitable, violent conflict.

In general, I believe that the Zealots would have most closely identified with the Pharisees — both choosing to lift up the Law of Moses above the Roman rule, but the Zealots chose to compromise more for political power rather than focusing on the spiritual aspect the way the Pharisees leaned. They both chose to remain in the public sector and fight, rather than flee, the Roman Occupation. However, I believe when it came to the problem of innocent bystanders, the Zealots actually shared a bit in common with the Essenes.

Both the Zealots and the Essenes accepted the loss of some Jewish people for the sake of maintaining cultural identity. This may stem from something we might call the Remnant Theology — or the belief that God will not deliver all His people, but that there will always be a select few, who are typically considered "pure," whom God will protect, deliver, and bless with victory and a return to authority. The Old Testament Prophets are filled with passages that follow an outline of:

1. Accusation against the people

2. Judgment and consequences of their sin

3. Hope given for mercy and future blessing

These passages are still today read in community and national perspectives that foster that kind of Remnant Theology. This perhaps is where the Pharisees and Zealots might travel along different paths. The Pharisees focused in on reading and interpreting the Law of Moses. The Zealots (and the Essenes) put their focus upon the Prophets. I do not think this is an issue of right/wrong. If we value the Scripture as a whole, and if we follow the example of Jesus, we notice that He is as at home with the Law and the Prophets both, as well a quite conversant in the Psalms and Writings that occur in between the two ends.

In fact, in regard to this Remnant Theology, Jesus shows an example that is curious. He does choose a select remnant, to minister to and to train to lead God's Kingdom. Yet He also does not refuse the nameless crowd that gathers around Him seeking healing, provision, and guidance. I think if there is any delineation to be made between the chosen Remnant and the rest of the general population, it is not based upon salvation, healing, deliverance, or provision. It is on the subject of leadership... and authority. Jesus, has a willingness to help everyone, but only a remnant will be chosen to share His authority in God's kingdom.

So how does Jesus deal with these people in authority? He shakes things up.

Mark chapter 2 shows the genius of Jesus in tying together spiritual problems, disease, and authority. As Jesus is preaching, a paralyzed man is brought before Him. Jesus, who has already healed many at this point, does not pronounce healing, but instead pronounces forgiveness of sin. Knowing the thoughts of the religious authorities in the room with Him, Jesus asks:

Why do you question these things in your hearts? 9Which is easier, to say to the paralytic, 'Your sins are forgiven,' or to say, 'Rise, take up your bed and walk'? 10But that you may know that the Son of Man has authority on earth to forgive sins"--he said to the paralytic-- 11"I say to you, rise, pick up your bed, and go home.34"

Everyone was amazed as the man picked up his mat and walked out of the house. This is something key about understanding the authority that Jesus has. It is holistic. It is pervasive. Jesus is not just the Lord of Sunday morning — He is the Lord of every day and everything in between. He does not just command the angels — even the demons must obey His commands. His rule is not just political and economic — it is spiritual, it is physical, and it touches every aspect of our lives.

That kind of authority was challenging and threatening to those who wielded only a small measure of authority over certain areas of life. Generally, these kinds of people would fight desperately to maintain the small amount of authority they obtained. Jesus did not have to fight for His authority, though. It was God-given.

The rest of Mark's gospel can be read with this repetition of Jesus challenging the powers in this world:

Jesus challenges the spiritual rule of sin and evil spirits.

Jesus challenges the physical rule of disease and injury (and death).

Jesus challenges the political rule of those wielding earthly authority.

The examples just keep rolling out through the pages of this gospel, often tied together by the teaching Jesus gives to his disciples and the questions He asks and answers of the religious authorities. This is how Jesus conquers. This is how God takes back a nation. He focuses on the spiritual problems, deals with the physical ramifications, and then sets up a chosen leadership to share in this

---

34 The Holy Bible: English Standard Version. (2001). (Mk 2:8–11). Wheaton: Standard Bible Society. [The Holy Bible: English Standard Version. (2001). (Mk 2:8–11). Wheaton: Standard Bible Society.]

work.

I do not expect the Zealots would have had a problem with the first four fishermen disciples, although I expect they all interacted with the Romans more than the Zealots would have approved. But the next disciple selected, Levi, would have given them fits. Levi was a tax collector, which meant he took money from the Jews and gave it to the Roman government. At best, if Levi was an honest tax collector and did not use fraud to earn extra profit himself, he would still have been considered a traitor to the nation and public enemy number two on the Zealot's hit list. Yet Jesus chose him to be one of the elite leaders of the Christian movement. Why? Because the holistic authority of Jesus was able to turn enemies into allies. That is how Jesus used his political authority.

Jesus not only held that authority with more security than either the Romans or the Jews, but He lived it out with a greater responsibility that traced back to the times of David, the man after God's own heart, who led Israel into some of their finest years as a nation. This authority Jesus showed, as the King of kings may be best represented in His relationship to the Crowd.

The King and the Crowd

The Role of King

In Deuteronomy 17:14–20,

> "...God announces that he intends Israel to have a king some day. He also specifies what the characteristics of a good king would be: (1) someone chosen by Yahweh; (2) a native Israelite; (3) one who doesn't spend his ambition multiplying horses, wives or money; (4) and one who will 'write for himself a copy of this law on a scroll in the presence of the Levitical priests' and read it every day of his life.[35]

Israel's desire for a king at the end of the time of Judges did not surprise God, nor was it outside His plan for them. However, God

---

[35] Richter, S. L. (2008). *The Epic of Eden: A Christian Entry into the Old Testament* (p. 195). Downers Grove, IL: IVP Academic.

had some specific criteria for the person who would claim the throne of Israel. These criteria went well beyond being a native Israelite. God wanted someone who would let God lead.

David has been heralded as the closest to perfect king that Israel ever had. In fact, after a bad experience with their first king, Saul, the royal family was swapped out for the house of the youngest son of Jesse of Bethlehem — a boy not coming from wealth, but rather from the background of a shepherd. I think it is no coincidence that God chose a shepherd to be king, because the role of an Israelite king and a shepherd are nearly identical.[36]

The first job of a shepherd is to keep the sheep safe and healthy. The first role of a king is to keep their people safe and healthy. If the country is under attack or beset by disease, the kingdom will dissolve and there will be no need for a king. David demonstrated this when he fought the Philistines on behalf of Israel and king Saul. He was willing to put his life on the line to protect his people.

We have already witnessed the way Jesus demonstrated this as well in Mark's gospel — by immediately confronting the evil spirits that were prevalent in the country and by healing everyone who came to him of their disease and injury. David was a good shepherd to Israel, and Jesus is the Good Shepherd to us all. In this way, Jesus demonstrates His first qualification as a king.

The second job of the shepherd is to keep the sheep fed. Probably the best Old Testament example of this is Joseph from Genesis 41-47. Joseph is not technically a king, but he is the second in command to Pharaoh (who actually functions a little more in the role God chooses to play over Israel). Joseph's main duties, particularly in light of the upcoming famine, are to make sure everyone as enough food to eat. At a national level, this kind of care-giving takes on more of an administrative role than we typically expect out of shepherds. The basic concept remains the same, though. Keep your sheep or people fed.

The easiest illustration of Jesus feeding people is from his account feeding the 5,000 in Mark 6:30. After the death of John the Baptist,

---

[36] (Richter and Richter, 2008, pp. 206–207)

Jesus was followed by 5,000 people out of town to listen to His teaching. Evening came, and the crowd was too far from home to make it back to eat, and they had brought very little among themselves to eat there. In Mark's account, Jesus tells the disciples to feed them — perhaps as a beginning to the roles they will take on as future shepherds of God's people. They gather up five loaves of bread and two fish and Jesus feeds the entire crowd with it, with twelve baskets of food left over.

Mark also makes an unusual connection between Jesus, David, feeding your flock, and the Sabbath traditions. At the end of Chapter 2, the disciples of Jesus were plucking heads of grain in a grain field they passed through. The Pharisees complain to Jesus that these disciples are breaking the Sabbath traditions.

> *"Have you never read what David did, when he was in need and was hungry, he and those who were with him: how he entered the house of God, in the time of Abiathar the high priest, and ate the bread of the Presence, which it is not lawful for any but the priests to eat, and also gave it to those who were with him?" And he said to them, "The Sabbath was made for man, not man for the Sabbath. So the Son of Man is lord even of the Sabbath."[37]*

The Old Testament reference Jesus alludes to here is not one of setting a new standard, but more of an exception to a general rule. Jesus explains that this is because the Pharisees misunderstand the purpose of this law.[38] The Sabbath law was not created so that people would be burdened. It was made so that they would have an opportunity to be unburdened. Imagine being a slave in a majority-world country. You would be doing hard labor from the moment you woke up until the moment you laid down to sleep. Your life would be nothing but work. God's Sabbath law was created to give people like that the freedom to rest one day a week, and also to ensure that they were given opportunity to learn about and worship God. The Sabbath law is meant to be a blessing, not a hindrance.

---

[37] *The Holy Bible: English Standard Version.* (2001). (Mk 2:25–28). Wheaton: Standard Bible Society.
[38] See Chapter 1 in Matthew.

That leads to the final role of being a king in Israel: keeping your people faithful to God. This is both the simplest and most difficult task of all. It is simple because it always begins and ends with the king being a faithful servant to God. There is no way around this, although it has been tried countless times. An unfaithful leader cannot lead people into faithfulness. The king is always first citizen of God's kingdom and therefore lives as an example of what that citizenship looks like.

Communicating *what* to do is fairly simple, but communicating *why* to do it is more challenging, especially to a large crowd of people. Does it matter if people know the "why" as long as they are doing what they are supposed to be doing? Absolutely! If I do not understand the value of doing something, I will only continue doing it as long as there is an outside motivation in my life. As soon as a new wave comes along that tells me there is another "right" way to do something, I will change and will have no reasons to resist that change other than the authority of the persons telling me what to do. I will simply revert back or follow the new latest thing. When my leader does not communicate their values and motivations for making choices, it takes the thinking out of my hands. It does not make me a mindless slave or absolve me of responsibility, but I cannot very well pass on to others values and motivations that I do not have or do not know about myself. I cannot be expected to use my thoughts accurately to determine if and when to change my actions. You have to communicate the "why."

Communicating the "why" is part of how the spiritual leaders of Israel were supposed to keep God's people faithful. Take Moses for example. He could have written the Ten Commandments and a handful of worship regulations and been done with his part in the Old Testament. Instead, he chose to tell the Hebrew story of deliverance from Egypt and to constantly remind the people that the reason they were to obey these new laws was to keep them from ending up as slaves of another nation again and outside God's favor. There were five books written to that account with commands to continually read and tell that story over and over again, but the Hebrew people still struggled to communicate the "why" over the generations. It is even possible that the four types of Jews only existed in the first century because they had not all received the same "why" regarding the law, and so all took different perspectives and interpretations of it. It might be true of the Church today: that we exist in hundreds of different forms largely because our own predecessors did not pass on the "why" to us.

David probably communicated all of this best in his famous Psalm 23. The prayer-song we teach our children and read at funerals because it brings us comfort and is filled with beautiful imagery is every bit as much a pledge of allegiance to God and a description of what true biblical authority looks like. It looks like a shepherd — one who keeps his flock safe, keeps them fed, and keeps them close to their God in the middle of a world going crazy all around them.

Let us look next to Jesus, who did not write about being a Good Shepherd, but lived it out as an example instead.

Jesus and the Crowd

Jesus delivered the people from evil spirits and healed them from illness and injury. He fed them. He also taught them how to stay faithful to God in all they do. He was their Good Shepherd in word and in deed, and He trained His disciples to do the same. But how did his flock treat Him? This is the question that I think turns the tides in this gospel and truly makes it of political interest.

The crowd had a polarized relationship with Jesus, largely based on self-interest. The crowds gathering to follow Jesus were small at first buildup was gradual at first. Four fishermen and a tax collector. By the time John the Baptist had died though, Jesus was being followed by thousands. This crowd waxed and waned a bit depending on the region Jesus was in and whether or not He was performing healings and other miracles or teaching the ins and outs of being part of God's kingdom. In short, the crowds loved the spectacle and benefits of the miracles, but many turned away and went home when Jesus started talking about commitment. Family and cultural values often outweighed their dedication to God. When the safety and security of the followers was put in jeopardy, many were willing to betray Jesus and hand him over for execution.

This relationship with the crowd culminates in Mark (and in all the gospels) with His final entry to Jerusalem. In Chapter 11, Jesus rode into Jerusalem on a colt and the crowds waved palm branches and covered the road with their cloaks. They were shouting:

> *"Hosanna! Blessed is he who comes in the name of the Lord! Blessed is the coming kingdom of our father David! Hosanna in the highest!*[39]*"*

This was an overtly political statement. This was the gospel — the "good news" of the crowd. They saw someone who had the credentials, the character, and the power to take back their country and they were marching to the capitol with Jesus, as they believed He was going to take back the political power from Rome and free them from Roman occupation. This was their Independence Day!

I can only imagine the excitement and tension within the hearts and minds of those with Zealot leanings as they saw Jesus ride into town that day. There was so much potential and so much at stake. If Jesus could cast out Rome the way He cast out evil spirits, then this would be a victorious day indeed. However, if something went wrong, they feared an unprecedented backlash from the Roman Empire that could cost thousands of lives and eradicate their cultural heritage forever.

That fear had an important basis. Rome was officially a polytheistic (worshiping many gods) empire that allowed the worship of most any god, so long as the Emperor was worshiped as well. It was a good political compromise that allowed them to keep the peace in many of their colonies while maintaining their authority. The single exception to this rule was the Jews. The Jews enjoyed a special status that allowed them to be monotheists (worshiping only one "true" god) and not being forced to worship the emperor. They enjoyed this privilege for good behavior and either supporting Rome or abstaining from politics altogether. In other words, Rome had decreed that is was not polite to mix religion and politics unless it was <u>Roman </u>religion and politics. Those who were not polite were treated with extreme prejudice and often made into examples for the rest of the Empire as to how Rome dealt with her enemies. I think all of this is important to bear in mind when we read that Jesus did

---

[39] *The Holy Bible: English Standard Version.* (2001). (Mk 11:9–10). Wheaton: Standard Bible Society.

not march that parade to the Roman governor's house, nor to the palace of king Herod. Instead He took that crowd and marched to the Temple.

Instead of cleaning up the Roman government and casting out the traitorous Jews who traded their loyalty for political power, Jesus went to clean out the Temple and to cast out those who made their living trying to help people worship God. In all his time in Jerusalem (and throughout his entire ministry), Jesus never criticized the Roman authorities. In fact, the only time He even speaks about their authority is not done as a criticism of Rome, but of the disciples. John and James approached Him seeking honor and authority in the new kingdom they saw Jesus building around them and asked to sit at his right and left hand. Jesus replied:

> *"You know that those who are considered rulers of the Gentiles lord it over them, and their great ones exercise authority over them. But it shall not be so among you. But whoever would be great among you must be your servant, and whoever would be first among you must be slave of all. For even the Son of Man came not to be served but to serve, and to give his life as a ransom for many.[40] "*

For Jesus, it was not merely about who was right and who was wrong. It was about God's people being called to live by a higher standard. Not a right and more right, but passable and those leading the way. That was why Jesus did not start by confronting the government. He started by confronting the spiritual leaders of God's people, whose jobs were to be beacons of light, leading the way for everyone — Jews and Gentiles alike!

That really messed the people up. The final straw was that, instead of Jesus calling for the destruction of the government institutions, He told the people that their temple would be destroyed — not one stone laying on another — and that three days later it would be raised again. That statement not only let the air out of his campaign popularity, it popped it completely. It was at this point in the narrative that Judas began to make plans to betray Jesus.

---

[40] *The Holy Bible: English Standard Version.* (2001). (Mk 10:42–45). Wheaton: Standard Bible Society.

The King and the Cross

Jesus foretells His death three times between Peter's confession of Him as the Christ and Christ's final entry into Jerusalem.[41] He did nothing to incite this kind of execution from the government, reserved for criminals who had demonstrated themselves to be enemies of Rome. As noted above, His criticisms were retained for the Jewish leaders and occasionally His own disciples. His arrest inspired one disciple to cut the ear off one of those sent to arrest Jesus — imagine how many of them might have been willing to lay down their lives for Him if He had confronted the Romans instead of the Jews. There must have been so much confusion among the disciples who heard Jesus predict His death and resurrection and march into Jerusalem like this was all according to plan.

I think it must have been even worse for the crowds that may not have heard those predictions, but only saw Him facing the wrong enemy once He got into town. They did not want a spiritual reformer, at least not immediately. They wanted political reform first. The Zealots may be best represented by these crowds as a group and perhaps by Judas Iscariot as an individual. They ran hot or cold about Jesus and were motivated by their own self-seeking agenda. When they discovered that Jesus was not going to deliver them from Rome, they turned on Him. It was these crowds, not the Romans, and perhaps not even really the Jewish leaders who sent Jesus to the cross.

Why the crowds and not the Jewish leaders? The Pharisees did not have the influence with the government to get it done, and in this case, the Sadducees did not either. They had to "stir up" the crowd to get the deed done. After the governor Pilate interrogated Him and Jesus refused to defend Himself, Pilate tried to have Him pardoned. Mark writes:

> *Now at the feast he used to release for them one prisoner for whom they asked. And among the rebels in prison, who had committed murder in the insurrection, there was a man called Barabbas. And the crowd came up and began to ask Pilate to do as he usually did for them. And he answered them, saying, "Do you want me to release for you the King*

---

41 Mark 8:27-30; Mark 11.

of the Jews?" For he perceived that it was out of envy that the chief priests had delivered him up. But the chief priests stirred up the crowd to have him release for them Barabbas instead. And Pilate again said to them, "Then what shall I do with the man you call the King of the Jews?" And they cried out again, "Crucify him." And Pilate said to them, "Why, what evil has he done?" But they shouted all the more, "Crucify him." So Pilate, wishing to satisfy the crowd, released for them Barabbas, and having scourged Jesus, he delivered him to be crucified.[42]

Who did Pilate wish to satisfy with this crucifixion? The crowd. In the place of Jesus, Pilate released Barabbas, whose description matches the Zealots party line completely. So how did Jesus interact with the Zealots and the crowd? He refused to fight their political battles at all and instead stuck with His own agenda. He chose spiritual reformation over political reformation. He spent His efforts healing and feeding those in need, not fighting and allowing them to become innocent casualties. He invited them to follow Him. They in turn, received all of that with open arms, and then, when they realized He would not be their secret weapon against Rome, betrayed Him, and demanded Rome do their worst to Him. How did Jesus interact with the Zealots and the crowd? He died for them — literally in their place. He took the death from Rome that they would have suffered.

How do we respond to the enemy?

The politics of Mark is wrapped up in identifying our enemies and showing how to respond to them. Jesus made his agenda clear in how He prioritized those stumbling blocks to God's reign in this world. He always placed the spiritual matters above the worldly ones — striking at the root of the problems rather than the consequences. He then immediately followed up with a healing of the brokenness and consequences of sin and spiritual warfare. Remember the healing of the paralyzed man? Jesus demonstrated that real authority embraces both the physical and spiritual but chooses to start with the spiritual. Unlike the others around Him who sought authority in the world around them, Jesus exercised authority first over Himself.

---

[42] *The Holy Bible: English Standard Version.* (2001). (Mk 15:6–15). Wheaton: Standard Bible Society.

From the beginning to the end of the gospel account, surrounded by enemies on all sides, Jesus always exemplified *self-control*.

This is a challenge set to our world today and our church in particular. For most of the 20th century, the Church was largely divided into two branches: Conservative and Liberal. These two branches were identified by their interaction with the poor and oppressed. Conservatives preached to them and tried to get them "saved," while the Liberals tried to help them physically. Toward the end of the 20th century, most churches began to realize that it takes both (and most of these denomination roots began doing both).

What does it mean to prioritize the spiritual aspects of helping others? Does it mean that if someone refuses spiritual intervention we should turn them away from seeking physical help? Of course not! Jesus healed many people who never followed Him or became disciples. The importance of His ministry was never what the disciples did or how the crowd responded — the importance was always in what Jesus offered. Prioritizing the spiritual simply means that we must offer spiritual help and not just physical.

How does that work in a nation fixated on the separation of church and state? It won't. Unless the government takes up Christ and receives His power to work in our broken places, effectively adopting a state religion, they cannot care for the spiritual needs of their people. They might be able to keep them safe and they might be able to keep them fed, but they cannot keep them faithful to God. A closer look at the way Jesus had that authority over His Kingdom showed that even in the areas of protection and provision, Jesus always connected those tasks to faithfulness to God. I'm not advocating the adoption of a state religion, but I am stating that I believe the government is not set to care for the spiritual needs of the people and will always have to ask the church for help in that.

That creates an awkward place of shared authority that we have been living in throughout the history of the United States. It means people will try to take sides with either the government or the church and try to put them at odds with one another, even when they are not really in conflict. It is like two workers building a bridge, one on each side, hoping to meet each other in the middle. If neither side communicates, the bridge will likely not line up right, because what you perceive on the other side is not always what is actually being built there. However, if both builders share their notes, collaborate, perhaps even take turns working on both sides with one another, there will be a unified vision and the project will be completed perfectly. That is the difference between delegation and true teamwork. Jesus does not call us to delegate some work to the government and some work to the church. He calls for teamwork, and, for teamwork to be possible, we have to exercise self-control and not be goaded or manipulated into political polarization.

Why do I think that? Because Jesus did not criticize the government. He criticized the religious leaders who had adopted the same kinds of attitudes of the government. God put the Church in place, not to delegate things away to other agencies or to dictate what should be done in the world, but to be a witness. Jesus gave His disciples authority and power, and a job to do after His resurrection, but it was not to be accomplished by compulsion or coercion. It was to be accomplished the same way He did it: by being a witness to the love and power of God. Jesus claimed that authority over His enemies in Jerusalem, not by raising a hand or even raising words of accusation against them. He won authority in their hearts and lives when He picked up His cross, walked to Calvary, took all their wrath, and gave His life for them. "And when the centurion [the government representative], who stood facing him, saw that in this way he breathed his last, he said, 'Truly this man was the Son of God!43'"

The crucifixion of Christ reveals the rot at the core of the Zealot's political beliefs of taking back political power by any means necessary. But how can you make political change by forgiving your enemies and dying in their place? That flies in the face of any sense of self-preservation! Ask Mahatma Ghandi or Dr. Martin Luther King, Jr... ask Archbishop Oscar Romero and Elizabeth Elliot. Why don't you ask St. Patrick, who led one of the most celebrated missionary efforts in Ireland, to the very people who had enslaved him as a young boy? When you focus on spiritual reform and invite in political reform — when the church steps up to be the Church

---

43 *The Holy Bible: English Standard Version.* (2001). (Mk 15:39). Wheaton: Standard Bible Society.

God calls them to be and invites the rest of the world in by serving them and making room for them, then, and only then, will you find political reform with the power to redeem generations and inspire those beyond the border of your own nation. Jesus forever changed the methods of political revolution by changing the question from, "What would you fight for?" to "Who would you give up your life for?"

So, who would you give up your life for, and do you have the self-control to give up your life for those who would stand against you?

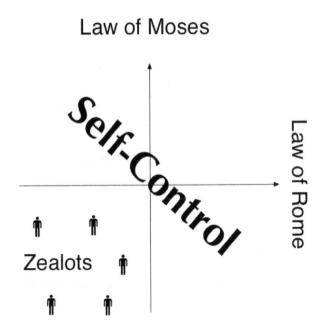

Chapter Five
The Sadducees and The Gospel of Luke-Acts

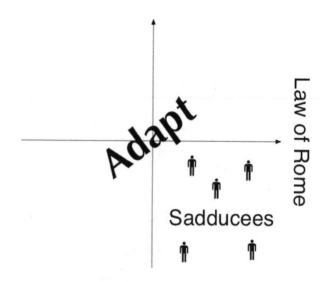

Sadducees: Liberal Jews

If the Pharisees of Jesus' day were the conservative Jews, then the Sadducees may have represented the liberal Jews. Since the labels of conservative and liberal have changed over the years, it may be more helpful to specify what those values were.

Both the Pharisees and Sadducees valued the Scripture. The Sadducees, however, placed a greater value on the Torah — the first five books of the Jewish Bible, sometimes referred to as "The Law of Moses." To them, the first five books were the words of God and the rest of the scripture was commentary. They held less regard for the prophets than the Pharisees, perhaps because the prophets spoke more of judgment of those in power and made more allusions to resurrection than are found in the Torah. Since they were the Jewish leaders in power, those prophecies may not have set well with them.

There is another reason why they placed more value on the Torah. It contained their job descriptions. The Torah set up the method of worship for all the Israelites and placed certain people, even certain families, in charge of responsibilities within that worship system. There were many animal sacrifices and food offerings to make. There was property and utensils to maintain. The Law of Moses also needed to be taught and passed on to the next generations. In short, working at the Temple in Jerusalem was a business, and, in some cases, a family business. The Sadducees were dedicated to making sure this business of theirs, which they truly saw as one of the most important cultural aspects of the Jewish people, would survive under Roman Oppression.

Liberal theology, in the first century Jewish context, was a little past "God helps those who help themselves" and moving much more into something like deism, which says that God created the world and got it started, now it is our job to keep it going.

Why would you be a Sadducee?

Scripture tells us only a couple things about the Sadducees.

1. They did not believe in the resurrection.[44]

2. They had significant influence in the Temple in Jerusalem.[45]

What is important about this belief in the resurrection? For the Jews, resurrection was not just about life after death. Their concept of the resurrection involved the judgment of all people in the world at the end of days by God. Some will be rewarded for their faithfulness. Others will be punished for disobedience. At the center of this judgment will be the one they call the Messiah. You see, for the Jews, the Messiah was not just about saving their own skin (or souls); the

---

[44] Matthew 22:23; Mark 12:18-27; Acts 23:8
[45] Acts 4:1 and Acts 5:17

Messiah was about bringing justice upon the heads of their enemies, as well. In their minds, you don't get one without the other.

Rome was not fond of the idea of a foreign God from a little backwater nation like Israel judging them, let alone punishing them. This was exactly the kind of preaching that would get you executed quite quickly. In fact, the Jews were already facing serious challenges of atheism within the Roman Empire. Rome, in general, was fairly tolerant of other religious. They only had two rules:

1. You had to honor the emperor.

2. You had to worship something with a visible representation.

This was a major problem for the Jews, because God had forbidden them to worship anyone besides Him or make any physical representation of Him as far back as the Law of Moses. Essentially Rome was demanding that they break the first two commandments of the Law. So someone decided to try to come to a compromise with the Romans, perhaps one of the Sadducees. This compromise would never work while they still held on to this belief about a coming resurrection and judgment and a Messiah who would lead it all. That kind of preaching would bring down the wrath of the Roman army upon their heads and wipe the Jewish nation off the map forever, thus ending the worship of the one true God. So a compromise was struck, and I believe it was one that has persisted even to the Liberal Jews of our day. They de-personalized the Messiah.

Perhaps after 500 years without hearing from God, the Sadducees began to wonder if all this waiting for the Messiah to come was just in vain. Rather than doubt God's power or care for them, they began to wonder if they misunderstood what the Messiah was going to be. Someone asked, "What if the Messiah is not a person at all?" They put their minds and imaginations to work, and eventually some decided that maybe the Messiah was a period of time, or in a way, a generation of people who would finally grow and mature into God's true, faithful believers, and justice would be done across the entire world. The "Messiah" would be a golden age for the Jews.

For this to happen, the Jewish culture needed to survive, and I believe there was a little bit of divine genius to this theological leap they made. By compromising and building bridges with Rome (who was very religiously inclusive), they might actually be a positive influence upon the Empire and convert these Gentiles from the inside of their government out. There was a mission opportunity for them, if they could find a way to coexist for the moment. This was not entirely out of line with the spirit and purpose of the Law of Moses either. They could look back to Exodus, to the founding of the Law and read:

> *Now therefore, if you will indeed obey my voice and keep my covenant, you shall be my treasured possession among all peoples, for all the earth is mine; and you shall be to me a kingdom of priests and a holy nation. These are the words that you shall speak to the people of Israel.[46]*

Under the stress of Roman occupation, the Sadducees chose to reframe the question of "fight or flight" to "adapt or die." The Sadducees chose to adapt.

Adapt or Die?

The Sadducees had a two-pronged approach to survival. Their defensive tactic was to water down the doctrine enough to appear tame enough for Rome to leave alone. Over time, this grew and spread into new applications. E. Stapfer writes:

> But the Sadducees are those that compose the second order, and take away fate entirely, and suppose that God is not concerned in our doing or not doing what is evil; and they say, that to act what is good or what is evil is at man's own choice, and that the one or the other belongs so to everyone, that they may act as they please. They also take away the belief of the immortal duration of the soul and the punishments and rewards in Hades. Moreover, the Pharisees are friendly to one another, and are for the exercise of concord and regard for the public; but the behaviour of the Sadducees one towards another is in some

---

[46] *The Holy Bible: English Standard Version.* (2001). (Ex 19:5–6). Wheaton: Standard Bible Society.

> degree wild, and their conversation with those that are of their own party is as barbarous as if they were strangers to them. And this is what I had to say concerning the philosophic sects among the Jews.[47]"

If there is no belief in ultimate judgment, then anything becomes permissible. This led to the second approach, a more offensive approach to dealing with Rome: the accumulation of wealth. Along with the Greek language used in business across the Roman Empire, Rome introduced the universal language of wealth. *Anything* could be bought for the right price. Roman nobility titles were bought and sold. The kings of the nations of the Roman Empire acquired and kept those thrones through wealth given to Rome. If the flow of money stopped coming to Rome, those rulers were deposed, and new ones were placed who would return the flow of profit to the Empire. That meant that not only could the Jews win the favor of Rome by taming their doctrines and putting them more in line with the Roman culture, they could actually buy that favor with actual wealth, ensuring their survival and actually giving them power and influence over the society.

This opportunity however, became their snare as the quest for survival of their people became a quest for personal power. I think this is no better illustrated than by Luke himself as he describes the way the devil attempted to make Jesus a Sadducee just before He began his ministry:

> *And Jesus, full of the Holy Spirit, returned from the Jordan and was led by the Spirit in the wilderness for forty days, being tempted by the devil. And he ate nothing during those days. And when they were ended, he was hungry.*

> *The devil said to him, "If you are the Son of God, command this stone to become bread." And Jesus answered him, "It is written, 'Man shall not live by bread alone.'"*

> *And the devil took him up and showed him all the kingdoms of the*

---

[47] Stapfer, E. (1885). *Palestine in the Time of Christ.* (A. H. Holmden, Trans.) (Third Edition, pp. 311–312). New York: A. C. Armstrong and Son.

world in a moment of time, and said to him, "To you I will give all this authority and their glory, for it has been delivered to me, and I give it to whom I will. If you, then, will worship me, it will all be yours." And Jesus answered him, "It is written, "'You shall worship the Lord your God, and him only shall you serve."'

And he took him to Jerusalem and set him on the pinnacle of the temple and said to him, "If you are the Son of God, throw yourself down from here, for it is written, "'He will command his angels concerning you, to guard you,' and 'On their hands they will bear you up, lest you strike your foot against a stone."' And Jesus answered him, "It is said, 'You shall not put the Lord your God to the test."' And when the devil had ended every temptation, he departed from him until an opportune time.[48]

The devil tempted Jesus to exercise His will and power over trusting God for the sake of self-preservation. He tempted Jesus to abandon faith in God in exchange for political power over not only the Jews, but the entire world. Finally, trying a back-door approach, the devil tried to get Jesus to prove God's faithfulness to this plan of salvation by *preventing* an act of Jesus.

This last temptation is a little more difficult to catch because it goes against a direct, logical approach to our understanding of what temptation is. Here the devil is not only trying to get Jesus to turn away from God's plan, he wants him simply to question it, and to test it out to be sure that God really is in control. This should not be such a surprise since this is the very kind of temptation that he used against Adam and Eve in the Garden of Eden ("Did God really say that?") and he knows that when we no longer trust God's truthfulness and integrity, he has broken our faith and made us vulnerable to manipulation. The devil was essentially asking Jesus to test just how important Jesus was to his plan, by putting himself in danger and waiting to see if— God would keep Him safe and alive to fulfill His role as Messiah.

These are exactly the pitfalls that the Sadducees fell into headfirst as they, though small in number, amassed wealth and power, and began

---

[48] The Holy Bible: English Standard Version. (2001). (Lk 4:1–13). Wheaton: Standard Bible Society.

to rule the Temple in Jerusalem as puppet leaders of Rome and (as Luke portrays here) as puppet leaders of the devil. For the sake of self-preservation, the opportunity to have power in their community, and perhaps even to test God and see if He really even cared as much as the scriptures claimed He did, the Sadducees gave up faithfulness to God and embraced a political and religious stance of trying to save Israel themselves.

A New Way

A New Hope Proclaimed

Luke begins his account of the good news with this opening statement:

> *Inasmuch as many have undertaken to compile a narrative of the things that have been accomplished among us, just as those who from the beginning were eyewitnesses and ministers of the word have delivered them to us, it seemed good to me also, having followed all things closely for some time past, to write an orderly account for you, most excellent Theophilus, that you may have certainty concerning the things you have been taught.[49]*

Luke specifically identifies his audience and his purpose for writing. This "account" is written to a person or group of people with a Greek name that means "lover of God" and is meant to reinforce previous teaching given to them. It is also important to note that Luke's gospel is just the first part of his story, which is followed up by the Acts of the Apostles, and both should be considered together as a single narrative as well as separate works.

The narrative as a whole takes place over a much larger area than any of the other gospels — spanning from the road southwest to Ethiopia all the way through the Middle East, and eventually ends in the capitol of the Roman Empire itself. Even if we consider Luke's gospel apart from Acts, there are still significantly more references to Gentiles than the other gospels. Mark also has a longer

---

[49] *The Holy Bible: English Standard Version.* (2001). (Lk 1:1–4). Wheaton: Standard Bible Society.

introductory narrative, which includes two significant women, Elizabeth and Mary, the mothers of John the Baptist and Jesus, respectively. Unlike Matthew, Luke holds the entire birth narrative, pointing out the many prophecies fulfilled along the way. Luke's gospel account already begins with the presumption that God is still at work in the world through the power of the Holy Spirit, and many of these birth narrative prophecies are not Old Testament ones, but those given to the people just before and around the time of the birth of Jesus. Unlike Matthew, Luke takes his time getting to the genealogy of Jesus by pointing out all the ways that God is at work among His people, even in those darker days.

The genealogy, found in Luke 4:23-38, is unique as well. Matthew's gospel contains the only other genealogy, and it is used to specify Jesus as being from the line of King David and also to reaffirm His Jewish identity as a descendant of Abraham. Luke goes well past Abraham, though, in his genealogy, all the way back to Adam. Instead of identifying Jesus as a Jew and a son of Abraham, Luke identifies Him specifically as a "son of God." This sentiment will be echoed later through the gospel and Acts as the idea that Jesus is greater than Abraham, and those who follow Him — even if they are not of Abraham's Jewish lineage — will find themselves in a place connected with all humanity and connected to God. Luke takes the same story that we find in Matthew and tells it so that Jesus is not just king of the Jews, He is king of the entire world.

That is a liberal move, on par with the designs of the Sadducees, in their attempts to make the Jewish faith more palatable and perhaps relevant to the Roman Empire. The question is: is there any precedence for this move? Luke can arbitrarily report that the Holy Spirit spoke to all of those people during the birth narrative under the assumption that God still works and speaks in those times, but is there any historical basis to it, or are we simply taking Luke's word for it?

In chapter 4, following His time of temptation in the wilderness, Jesus began His ministry addressing that very question. He went to preach in His hometown of Nazareth, opened up the scroll of Isaiah 61 and read:

The Spirit of the Lord GOD is upon me,

because the LORD has anointed me
   to bring good news to the poor;
he has sent me to bind up the brokenhearted,
   to proclaim liberty to the captives,
and the opening of the prison to those who are bound;
   to proclaim the year of the LORD's favor,[50]

Then He closed the scroll and declared that this prophecy was fulfilled right then and there. The people were upset by this. Isaiah 61 is a prophecy of deliverance. It is a prophecy of the resurrection of the people and the judgment of their enemies — yet here they were, still under the rule of Rome. Nothing had changed. How could Jesus claim that this prophecy was fulfilled? They had heard stories of Jesus performing healings and miracles in Capernaum — a mixed Jewish/Gentile city in Galilee. Why had He not done anything like this in His hometown of Nazareth? So Jesus reminded them of the historical precedent in scripture for this.

In the time of the prophets, while Israel was divided by civil war and led by unfaithful leaders, Elijah, mightiest of God's prophets, did not perform miracles for anyone of the Jewish people, but instead went a widow named Zarephath of Sidon — a foreigner. Likewise, his disciple Elisha, when he took over as prophet, did not heal any of the Israelites, but instead healed Naaman the Syrian. Jesus pointed out that the mightiest prophets of old, if they exercised favoritism at all, exercised it on behalf of the Gentiles, not the Jews.

So Jesus proclaimed the fulfillment of one of the greatest prophecies in their midst and made the case that His miracles and healings given amongst the Gentiles rather than the Jews was based upon God's will in scripture. The Jews of His hometown, however, remained stuck in the same place they had been for the last 500 years — in the service of another nation. They were enraged, and a mob of them tried to kill Jesus that day by throwing Him off a cliff, but He passed through them and left. That may have been the first and last time Jesus visited His hometown once He began His preaching ministry.

---

[50] *The Holy Bible: English Standard Version.* (2001). (Is 61:1–2). Wheaton: Standard Bible Society.

A New Lesson Taught

In the book of Luke there are eleven parables that are not found in the other gospels:[51]

·Two Debtors (Luke 7:41-43)

·Good Samaritan (Luke 10:30-37)

·Importunate Friend (Luke 11:5-8)

·Rich Fool (Luke 12:16-21)

·Barren Fig Tree (Luke 13:6-9)

·Lost Piece of Silver (Luke 15:8-10)

·Lost Son (Luke 15:11-32)

·Unrighteous Manager (Luke 16:1-9)

·Rich Man and Lazarus (Luke 16:19-31)

·Unjust Judge (Luke 18:1-8)

·Pharisee and the Tax Collector (Luke 18:9-14)

These parables can be divided into two categories: those that affirmed the inclusive nature of the Sadducees and those that criticized their use of wealth.

Luke 15 contains some of the most well-known parables of Jesus, two of which are unique to Luke's gospel. The parables of the Lost Sheep (shared with Matthew), the Lost Coin, and their culmination in the parable of the Lost Son teach a unified truth between the three of them. Luke ends each parable with the repeated refrain,

> Just so, I tell you, there will be more joy in heaven over one
> sinner who repents than over ninety-nine righteous persons

---

[51] *The Companion Bible*, p. 1428.

who need no repentance.[52]

and

Just so, I tell you, there is joy before the angels of God over one sinner who repents.[53]

and finally,

It was fitting to celebrate and be glad, for this your brother was dead, and is alive; he was lost, and is found.[54]

Taken by themselves, these parables are probably best understood as being illustrations of God's love for His people. God does not desire that any should be lost. There is no immediate context to lead us to think Jesus is teaching about welcoming in the Gentiles yet through these parables. This instead would be heard as an affirmation to all the Jews, and to the Sadducees specifically for their work in providing a way of survival for all the Jews, not just the ones who "deserve" it, as their counterparts the Pharisees taught.

That affirmation ends there, though. Taking into account the wild lifestyles of some of the Sadducees, we might read the parable of the Lost Son as an allegorical tale depicting God as the Father of both the Pharisees (the elder son) and the Sadducees (the free-willed younger son). While it does, indeed, end with a welcome back home and celebration of the return of the Sadducee son, it also gives two important criticisms about wealth and the way they used it.

1. Wealth does not bring happiness, either in this life or the next.

2. God is willing to give up wealth for the sake of bringing home His lost children.

---

[52] *The Holy Bible: English Standard Version.* (2001). (Lk 15:7). Wheaton: Standard Bible Society.
[53] *The Holy Bible: English Standard Version.* (2001). (Lk 15:10). Wheaton: Standard Bible Society.
[54] *The Holy Bible: English Standard Version.* (2001). (Lk 15:32). Wheaton: Standard Bible Society.

The Sadducees, like the younger son were guilty of using God's wealth, which they gained through purchases and sacrifices made in the Temple, for their own gain. Jesus taught that it was only once they repented of that illicit use of wealth, trying to live life on their own, and returned back under the authority of God that they would truly find happiness.

Wealth was an important subject to the Jews, the early Christians, and to everyone else in the Roman Empire. While the Jews could not be born to Roman citizenship, they could use money to buy favor, keeping themselves safe and secure. But it was also a ruse, because you could never gain enough money to achieve any permanent status or safety. It was not the having of wealth, it was being a source of flowing wealth that the Empire rewarded, which meant that the Sadducees in the Temple could not just extort money from the Jews once and gain Roman favor — they had to set up ways to do it on a continual basis just to maintain their status.

The majority of these Luke-based parables are criticisms of the use of money in relation to the faithfulness of God and they are all very clear: you cannot trade faithfulness to God for money. Often in reading through these passages, we spiritualize them too quickly, comparing debts to sins; but in the eyes of the Sadducees, sins were the same as monetary debts. They ran the Temple, and that was the place where you traded money to buy sacrificial animals to be offered for the forgiveness of your sin. The more people sinned, the more money they made. It was not inherently wrong. They were simply offering a spiritual service to meet the needs of the Jewish people. God was not doing anything with the money. So they made a profit. It was the Sadducees who were accused of turning the Temple into a "den of robbers" instead of the "house of prayer" it was created to be.[55] What had begun as a sin of *omission* — failing to lead Israel into faithful relationship with God — grew into a sin of *commission* — making money off of their fellow Israelites and their need of forgiveness. All of this started with the thought that God just did not care about Israel anymore, that they were on their own. Jesus taught in these parables that the opposite was true. God did care. Indeed He cared enough to act beyond what appeared fair and right, giving sinners every chance to return home. God, to whom

---

[55] See Matthew 21:13; Mark 11:17; Luke 19:46.

everything is owed, paid the way for everyone else who could not afford to be a part of His kingdom. How did Jesus change this? How did Jesus change the den of robbers back into a house of prayer? Perhaps He did not.

Resurrection and the Holy Spirit

Choosing Death

The Apostle Paul would one day point back to the prophet Isaiah and call Christ a "stumbling block for the Jews."[56] It was specifically His crucifixion that would trip them up. All four types of Jews in Jesus day were completely baffled by everything that connected Jesus with the cross because it went against everything they had believed about themselves and about God.

The Sadducees had reframed the "fight or flight" dilemma into "adapt or die," and they were doing everything in their power to adapt to the new culture that grew up around them. Jesus refused to adapt. He held fast to the prophecy of the messiah who would lead them into freedom, despite the impossible odds. Political revolution was an impossibility against the Roman army. If the teachings of Jesus were not crazy enough in their high idealism, then His next move certainly was. They had followed Jesus, interviewed and interrogated Him. They had all done their best to try to win Him over as a champion to their side, but He refused to be swayed by anyone. Given the choice between adapt or die, Jesus chose to die.

Death chosen as a last resort is not unknown among political leaders throughout history. As Paul writes to the Christians in Rome, "For one will scarcely die for a righteous person — though perhaps for a good person one would dare even to die,"[57] and certainly many have given their lives in order to protect loved ones throughout time. What makes Jesus unique is that death was not the only option He was given. It was His first choice.

---

[56] 1 Corinthians 1:23; also Romans 9:33 and Isaiah 8:14
[57] *The Holy Bible: English Standard Version.* (2001). (Ro 5:7). Wheaton: Standard Bible Society.

Luke describes several opportunities Jesus has to choose an outcome other than the cross. After foretelling His death three times,[58] Jesus finally enters the city of Jerusalem for the last time. There He does several things to bring on the contempt of the Jewish leaders.

1. He kicks the merchants out of the Temple.

2. He confronts the Jewish leaders and refuses to explain His authority.

3. He tells some additional parables which call the religious leaders into question.

4. He dodges their trick questions about taxes and the resurrection.

5. He warns the crowd about the Jewish leaders and praises the poor.

6. He predicts the destruction of the Temple.

7. He predicts war and the destruction of Jerusalem.

8. He predicts the coming of the Messiah and the resurrection and judgment of the world.

9. He gives one last parable about knowing the times and warns them to be ready.[59]

Any one of these things might have put him on uneasy terms with the Jewish leaders, but predicting the destruction of the Temple and of Jerusalem was too much for them. Yes, these things were going to happen, but Jesus did not have to tell everyone about them. If He had just kept quiet, had a few little debates with the scribes and scholars, maybe did some preaching in the Temple, things might have been different. But Jesus went to town and let it all out.

It was at this point that He began to lose everybody, and it was here that He truly began to prepare for His death. He celebrated Passover with His disciples and explained His upcoming death to them

---

[58] Luke 9:21-22, 9:43-45, and 18:31, respectively.
[59] All from Luke 19:28-21:31

through that celebration. He then went to the garden of Gethsemane to pray. He explained to the disciples about their eventual betrayal and denial of Him, and how all of this fit into the prophetic plan God laid out centuries earlier. Just before His arrest in the garden, Jesus prayed for another way out, and this is the only time in the passion narrative we see Jesus even hint at changing course... but the exception here proves the rule, and He returns from prayer with even greater resolve as He meets Judas and those from the Jewish council, sent to arrest Him.

These were the active choices Jesus made to bring on His own death. The decisions that followed were more passive ones that simply allowed the momentum to continue to its ultimate conclusion. They were nearly all marked by silence from Jesus while He and His motives are questioned. At almost any point before being sentenced by Pilate, He could have recanted His preaching, apologized for the disturbance He had caused, or (at least in the presence of Pilate) simply defended Himself. It seems that whenever He was given an out He simply let it pass Him by, or said just enough to get things moving again toward the cross.

Choosing death is a bad move politically. It defies logic. It denies the most basic concept of self-preservation in the power-hungry politician. For the benevolent leader, it denies sustainability. It is well and good to want to change the world for the better, but if you choose not to stay around in it, how can it possibly continue in a good direction? The only way for you to make that choice is by having faith in something or someone beyond and perhaps greater than yourself. Jesus was able to see the cross as more than a choice for death — it was an act of sacrifice in obedience to God and for love of God's people.

If any of the politics of Jesus made sense to the Sadducees, or any of the Jewish leaders, they became lost the moment He set foot in Jerusalem and began making His way to the cross. They could not grasp how political death, let alone actual death, could lead to a victory for God's Kingdom.

Resurrection

The Resurrection of Jesus Christ was one of the most important political events in the history of the world. It was a game changer that forever redefined how people experienced leadership and freedom in our world, and every political regime that has followed has had to answer the question of how to respond to His resurrection.

Jesus changed the rules drastically. In monarchies, for example, civil wars have been fought over rights to succession to the throne. One of the greatest fears of people in those countries is getting caught between sibling rivals, both intent on being the ruler. The only thing worse than that is having a monarch with no heir at all, leaving the throne up for grabs to anyone who can take it and keep it.

When leadership passes down neatly, through plain processes, it is easier for those in power as well as those without. Why? Because that means the change that inevitably happens occurs slowly enough to be predictable. That gives those in power enough time to win over the upcoming monarch and the assurance that they can direct the oncoming change to their benefit. It also keeps the general population calmer because the change is not as drastic. If it happens slowly enough, it is not even noticeable. It works like boiling a frog. If you heat the water slow enough, the frog will simply cook to death; but if you heat it too quickly, the frog will become agitated and jump out. I've never cooked a frog before, but I have noticed that the most appreciated change for groups of people is certainly the one they don't even realize happened.

I'm sure there is a fear of losing control at the root of that distaste for change. There is a political equation that humanity bought into, perhaps back in the Garden of Eden,[60] that goes like this.

Power -> Control -> Freedom

Power leads to Control leads to Freedom, or so the story goes. If you want to experience freedom, you have to have control over your life. You cannot have control over your life without power. That is

---

[60] Genesis 3

the birth of politics right there.

When Jesus *chose* death, He gave up freedom, and control, and, therefore, it makes sense that He would lose power as well. He *chose* slavery when He had the power and the control to do whatever He wanted. The devil who ran this game on Adam and Eve tried to run it on Jesus, but failed, and here is how: the moment Jesus died on that cross, He was forever beyond the devil's reach. That is all well and good, so long as Jesus stays in the ground, or in the afterlife, in some other world. But that all fell apart when Jesus came back!

It is curious that something so as simple and singular as one man coming back from death would have such devastating effect upon the politic systems of our entire world... but think for a moment. If you knew for a fact that your death was only temporary, what would you have to fear? If you knew that you and all your loved ones would live forever while your enemies would be judged for their misdeeds, could anyone convince you to do something you did not want to do? Without the fear of death and punishment, governments lose their teeth and their ability to enforce any kind of law, good or bad. The most terrifying thing to an established government is a people without fear.

That is probably why they were so cruel to Jesus, mocking and beating him and asking for crucifixion rather than a quicker death. They needed to let everyone know that this behavior of His was madness and it was socially unacceptable. They needed to prove to themselves and everyone around Him that all this was a lie, that the world ran according to the Power/Control/Freedom formula and no other way. They could not imagine any other way. That was why the Jewish leaders had guards placed at the tomb, and why they bribed those guards after Jesus rose not to tell anyone.[61] The idea of resurrection, just the very idea of it, threatened the entire political establishment.

If the very idea of the resurrection was such a threat, can you imagine what kind of effect the actual event had? Can you imagine how the world was turned upside down for Peter, John, James, and all the

---

[61] Matthew 28:12-14

other disciples when they saw Jesus face to face? In choosing death, Jesus had defeated death, for Himself and any who followed Him, giving them freedom as a gift, not as something they had fight for themselves.

That was the political game changer. Because Jesus rose from the dead, and extended that invitation to join Him to anyone who was willing to follow, the world had to redefine the value of human life. Under the old system, it was simple. You were worth whatever benefits I could get out of you — no more, no less. But if we do not have death, or anything else to fear, and we find everything we need in Christ, there is no *need* to use one another. Systems of Quid Pro Quo break down, and we begin to talk about the value of human life, human dignity, and even human rights! We begin to see the possibility of what a world might look like if people were valued just because they were created by God, rather than on what I could get out of them.

Reggie Joiner spoke at a church conference two years ago and said that the most important truth we needed to grasp in order to lead in our communities was that every man, woman, and child was made in the image of God. They have worth before we ever meet them. God has invested the blood of His Son Jesus into these people whose value we may not be able to see ourselves. That is the truth that Jesus taught and the world rejected. That is the truth that He proved in His resurrection. That is the truth to which all the political systems in the world must respond.

How do our politics respond to the resurrection of Christ?

The Movement of the Holy Spirit

The resurrection could have been a one-time event that perhaps challenged the world, but ultimately left it detached when Jesus ascended into Heaven. After enough time had passed, a new religious order of Sadducees would have taken power and denied that Jesus ever existed in the first place. His followers would be wiped out or corrupted one by one until none were left, and the world would go back to running on schedule again. But that is not what happened.

Luke takes great pains to identify God at work in the world through the power of the Holy Spirit: before, during, and after the earthly life of Jesus. It was the Holy Spirit who brought prophecies to the people in the birth narrative of Jesus.[62] It was the Spirit which descended upon Jesus during His baptism and then led Him into the wilderness to be tempted by the devil.[63] Finally, it was the Holy Spirit which Jesus gave to His disciples and by which they became the Church — a community of the Kingdom of God, here on earth, and open to anyone who would receive it. Ultimately, it was this Holy Spirit that would guide the apostles until Jesus was being worshiped not only in Jerusalem, but throughout all the Roman Empire, even the capitol itself.

There is one final concept that I need to tie together regarding the politics of the Sadducees and the Holy Spirit: the transformation of the Temple.

The Gospel of Luke begins in the Temple and ends in the Temple.[64] Earlier I wrote about Jesus criticizing the Sadducees for turning God's Temple into a "den of robbers" and that Jesus may not have turned it back into a "house of prayer" for the nations of the world. To understand why not, we need to look at a small aside that Luke writes about during the death of Jesus. At the end of the crucifixion, Luke writes:

> It was now about the sixth hour, and there was darkness over the whole land until the ninth hour, while the sun's light failed. And the curtain of the temple was torn in two. Then Jesus, calling out with a loud voice, said, "Father, into your hands I commit my spirit!" And having said this he breathed his last.[65]

The curtain Luke refers to here is believed to be the special curtain that separated the Holy of Holies — the innermost sanctuary of the

62 Luke 1
63 Luke 4:1-13
64 Luke 1:5; 24:53
65 *The Holy Bible: English Standard Version.* (2001). (Lk 23:44–46). Wheaton: Standard Bible Society.

Temple — from the rest of the building.[66] Only the High Priest was allowed to meet God there and only after he had made himself ceremonially clean. This room held the Ark of the Covenant, and it was the one place the Jews believed God's presence rested while on earth. As its name aptly describes, it was their most sacred place and was to be separated and protected from the corruption of the common world.

Scholars believe this event can be interpreted in at least one of two ways. The first way is that the tearing of the curtain is a welcoming in of all people into God's presence. They believe that the sacrifice of Jesus on the cross gives everyone the same status as the spiritually purified High Priest, and allows us to approach the throne room of God.[67] The author of Hebrews may have been alluding to this when they wrote:

> *Therefore, brothers, since we have confidence to enter the holy places by the blood of Jesus, by the new and living way that he opened for us through the curtain, that is, through his flesh, and since we have a great priest over the house of God, let us draw near with a true heart in full assurance of faith, with our hearts sprinkled clean from an evil conscience and our bodies washed with pure water. Let us hold fast the confession of our hope without wavering, for he who promised is faithful. And let us consider how to stir up one another to love and good works, not neglecting to meet together, as is the habit of some, but encouraging one another, and all the more as you see the Day drawing near.[68]*

The second interpretation is that the tearing of the temple curtain was not an invitation of the world into the Holy of Holies, but rather the exit of God from it.[69] This carries some powerful implications with it. It implies a judgment upon Israel that was one of the primary punishments promised to them in the prophets as a result of their unfaithfulness — God taking His Spirit back from them. Why would

---

[66] See Leviticus 16.

[67] It should be noted that this interpretation is viewed primarily as symbolic of our ability to enter the heavenly Temple of God, for which the earthly Temple was just a pale imitation. If this were focused solely on the earthly Temple, this interpretation would have been made irrelevant by the destruction of the Temple that Jesus prophesied and which occurred in 70 AD.

[68] *The Holy Bible: English Standard Version.* (2001). (Heb 10:19–25). Wheaton: Standard Bible Society.

God choose that time and place to do that? Because they had just killed His Son Jesus.

There is some scriptural justification of this perspective from the Old Testament prophet Ezekiel who described a vision of God's throne being on wheels and moving about across the land.

> *Then the cherubim lifted up their wings, with the wheels beside them, and the glory of the God of Israel was over them. And the glory of the LORD went up from the midst of the city and stood on the mountain that is on the east side of the city. And the Spirit lifted me up and brought me in the vision by the Spirit of God into Chaldea, to the exiles. Then the vision that I had seen went up from me. And I told the exiles all the things that the LORD had shown me.*[69]

God's presence moves further and further out as the prophecy progresses, out of the Temple and out of Jerusalem — reaching out to the exiles in the nations surrounding them. It may be that the death of Christ marked the beginning of the judgment of Jerusalem as prophesied by Ezekiel. The implications for us, though, is not that those who were not worthy are now invited in, but instead that God left the unfaithful and sought out those who had not been worthy to approach Him. The difference in this second interpretation is that God comes to us, rather than waiting for us to come to Him.

Not only does the Temple (singular) become mobile in Luke's gospel, it also multiplies. The Holy Spirit began to move less frequently inside the traditional "sacred" area and more often in the "common" areas of life, with a clear direction toward Gentile territory. The place of God moves away from the base of the Sadducees into the territory of the Roman Empire.

A second structural indication of this contrast is evident in the early narrative of Acts.

---

[69] *The Holy Bible: English Standard Version.* (2001). (Eze 11:22–25). Wheaton: Standard Bible Society.

The Mission of the Holy Spirit

Luke's account of the Acts of the Apostles begins in a house and ends in a house, in contrast to the Temple as symbolic location in his gospel.[70] Neyrey writes:

> "Within the first eight chapters the scene shifts with regularity between the household, where the believers assemble, pray, receive the Spirit, break bread and generously share all things in common, and the temple as the center of political and religious control, a place for seeking alms, and the scene and object of conflict (arrest and imprisonment, critique of temple rulers, mob violence, beating, and death)"[71]

All four gospels refer to the Holy Spirit and tell a number of similar stories involving it. Luke however, is unique in that his records of the Spirit go beyond the ascension of Jesus and into the first decade of the Church. In fact, if you trace the movement of the Holy Spirit from the beginning of Luke's gospel to the end of the Acts of the Apostles, a certain pattern emerges.

1. The Holy Spirit prepares Israel for the birth of Jesus.

2. The Holy Spirit conceives Jesus.

3. The Holy Spirit leads the family of Jesus through His childhood.

4. The Holy Spirit leads Jesus through baptism, temptation, and beginning His ministry.

5. The Holy Spirit empowers Jesus to minister, suffer, and die on the cross.

6. The Holy Spirit tears the Temple curtain and/or leaves the Temple.

---

[70] Acts 1:12-13; 28:30
[71] Neyrey, 2000, p. 215

7. The Holy Spirit raises Christ from the dead.

8. The Holy Spirit is poured out upon the disciples to lead in the place of Christ.

9. The Holy Spirit is poured out upon Gentiles who become believers.

10. The Holy Spirit leads the church to move beyond Israel, making disciples all over the world.

There is a movement of the Spirit through Luke's writings, from the most sacred places of the Jews (both the Temple and Jesus Himself) to the common places of the Gentiles, until the Spirit is at work in the Capitol of Rome itself. Regardless of how we interpret the tearing curtain of the Temple, Luke points out that the Spirit moves out toward new places and new people. That should not be such a surprise either, since that is exactly what Jesus commanded in His final words to them:

> Then he said to them, "These are my words that I spoke to you while I was still with you, that everything written about me in the Law of Moses and the Prophets and the Psalms must be fulfilled." Then he opened their minds to understand the Scriptures, and said to them, "Thus it is written, that the Christ should suffer and on the third day rise from the dead, and that repentance and forgiveness of sins should be proclaimed in his name to all nations, beginning from Jerusalem. You are witnesses of these things. And behold, I am sending the promise of my Father upon you. But stay in the city until you are clothed with power from on high.[72]"

Underneath this change of locale is a subtler shift that is already anticipated among the Qumran (see next chapter). Perrin refers to the foreshadowing in Luke 3 and writes:

---

[72] *The Holy Bible: English Standard Version.* (2001). (Lk 24:44–49). Wheaton: Standard Bible Society.

94

"This judgment is further confirmed by his warning that 'God is able from these stones to raise up children to Abraham' (Luke 3.8). On consideration of this saying, whose authenticity is broadly granted, it bears stating that when Yahweh is described as 'raising up' (LXX: anistemi) something, that something is frequently either his 'offspring/seed' or the 'temple'. Moreover, when people in biblical literature are referred to as 'stones', it is regularly in reference to their capacity either as citizens of Israel or as temple members (if a distinction between these two roles can even be made).

The thrust of the Baptizer's pun, borrowed directly from scripture, is obvious: through John, God is raising up new children of Israel, who will also be constitutive of a new temple. Under the Baptizer, Israel is starting afresh, and with this new start comes, as a matter of course, a new temple.[73]"

The word "raise up" is the same word used for resurrection. In other words, through the power of the resurrection God is remaking His *people* into the building blocks of His new Temple.

Here is what is surprising. Do you recall the motives of the Sadducees? Not only did they have intentions of protecting the faith of God's people, but also in possibly promoting it throughout the Roman Empire by making it more acceptable to their standards. That was why they gave up belief in the resurrection and their hope in a messiah. They were hoping that perhaps the messiah would be a group of people in a "golden age" of the Jews yet to come. God accomplished all of that through Jesus the Messiah, who did not conquer by force but conquered by being crucified and then resurrected by the power of the Holy Spirit, and then gave that same Spirit to the body of His believers to become that very group of people and perhaps begin that very "golden age" for which the Sadducees were waiting. They were waiting on God, and He was right there in front of them, waiting on them.

So God, through His own promised methods, accomplished the best

---

[73] Perrin, 2010, p. 41

intentions of the Sadducees. He did so without seeking money, power, or safety. He did so not by fearing death, but by embracing it and transforming the world in the power of Christ's resurrection. What the Sadducees sought to win by compromise, Luke demonstrated that Jesus accomplished through faithfulness and sacrifice.

Where do we compromise in politics? Where do we demonstrate faithfulness to and trust in God in our politics?

Law of Moses

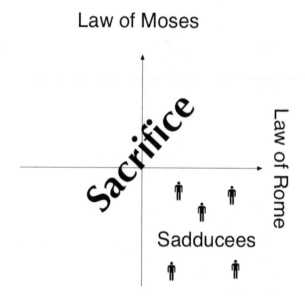

Chapter Six

The Essenes and the Gospel of John

Law of Moses

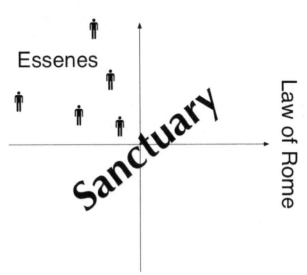

The Call

The Essenes: Qumran

The most famous example of the Jewish group called the Essenes was found at Qumran. Qumran was a community of Jewish people who had left the city life and created a new life for themselves faithfully following God in the wilderness area just west of the Dead Sea. There is no evidence to suggest they called themselves "Essenes" or that they were a unified group. Like the Zealots, these were probably smaller isolated groups of people drawn together by their common response to the oppression of the Roman Empire.

They lived in various communities throughout Palestine, but had a large settlement at Qumran. An initiation regime was required of all potential members: a preparatory period of study and examination was followed by two years of training, during which they were accepted in stages to share in the common property and the pure foods and drink. At some point, a solemn oath of loyalty was taken. A strict hierarchy, dominated by priests and elders, ordered their communities, led by individual fiscal and spiritual overseers, but judicial functions were carried out democratically by large bodies of full members. They held property in common but retained some personal discretion. Regularly (twice daily, according to Josephus., they shared a common meal over which a priest had to pray. Their purification baths were unique in that access was restricted to members of the sect alone after a probationary year, and purification was required before common meals as well as for the usual cases of impurity. They differed from the Temple authorities regarding cultic purity, and, therefore, seem to have restricted or renounced participation in sacrifices. Essenes carefully guarded certain esoteric knowledge, including the names of angels. Wealth was despised as a corrupting influence. They devoted themselves to the study of sacred writings. Transgressions of Mosaic laws and community rules were strictly punished by fines and expulsion. It is not certain that most Essenes were celibate or that they completely withdrew from all participation in the temple cult as is commonly believed.[74]

Although the gospels never refer to the Essenes, all four gospels give a description of a very influential person during the life of Jesus who may have been an Essene himself, or at least connected to them. That person was John the Baptist. John is identified as the cousin of Jesus and, perhaps more importantly, the prophet who prepared the way for His ministry. John's Gospel connects the purpose of John's preaching in the wilderness near the Jordan river to a passage from Isaiah that says:

> *A voice cries:*
> *"In the wilderness prepare the way of the LORD;*
> *make straight in the desert a highway for our God.*
> *Every valley shall be lifted up,*
> *and every mountain and hill be made low;*

---

[74] Falk, D. K. (1996). Essenes. In D. R. W. Wood, I. H. Marshall, A. R. Millard, J. I. Packer, & D. J. Wiseman (Eds.), *New Bible Dictionary* (3rd ed., pp. 340–341). Leicester, England; Downers Grove, IL: InterVarsity Press.

the uneven ground shall become level,
and the rough places a plain.
And the glory of the LORD shall be revealed,
and all flesh shall see it together,
for the mouth of the LORD has spoken.[75]

In Matthew and Luke, Jesus identifies John the Baptist as a prophet in the same spirit as Elijah:

> *Truly, I say to you, among those born of women there has arisen no one greater than John the Baptist. Yet the one who is least in the kingdom of heaven is greater than he. From the days of John the Baptist until now the kingdom of heaven has suffered violence, and the violent take it by force. For all the Prophets and the Law prophesied until John, and if you are willing to accept it, he is Elijah who is to come. He who has ears to hear, let him hear.*[76]

This tells us several important things about this fourth group of Jews. First, they lived off the grid and out of Roman influence as much as possible. We see this in the geography and conditions of where they lived. It is evident in their avoidance of anything considered unclean. It is portrayed in the monastic environment they created that focused all aspects of life on seeking God. We know there was a reverence for God's word because it was at the ruins of Qumran that we have found preserved fragments of some of the Old Testament prophetic writings. They apparently had a love of God and the Jewish culture and when Rome tried to impress Roman culture upon them, they simply left and formed new communities outside the influence or care of Rome.

This isolationism created a defensive attitude toward outsiders. Although there is some evidence of trade that occurred here,[77] there is also evidence that joining these communities was not easy. Multiple rights of purification were required, along with a

---

[75] *The Holy Bible: English Standard Version.* (2001). (Is 40:3–5). Wheaton: Standard Bible Society."
[76] *The Holy Bible: English Standard Version.* (2001). (Mt 11:11–15). Wheaton: Standard Bible Society.
[77] Falk, D. K. (1996). "Qumran." In D. R. W. Wood, I. H. Marshall, A. R. Millard, J. I. Packer, & D. J. Wiseman (Eds.), *New Bible Dictionary* (3rd ed., p. 1004). Leicester, England; Downers Grove, IL: InterVarsity Press.

probationary period, as noted above. They did not want just anyone entering in and bringing the pagan culture that these communities were trying so hard to fight against. For the Essenes, given the choice of fight or flight from Rome, they chose flight. Once they escaped, they were quick to fortify their defenses to prevent a further influx of Roman culture.

To the Essenes, culture and spirituality were intertwined. You could not claim to be a Jew but live by Roman standards. Life was not divided into separate spiritual and social categories, nor was there a difference between private and public. To them, all these were black and white issues. You either were in or you were out, and, before they welcomed you in, they wanted to be sure you were who you claimed you were. That is where the practice of baptism came in.

Baptism

Baptism, to the Jews, was a symbolic act that purified and freed them from gentile influence. In many ways, they believed in germs before the discovery of germs, although these "germs" they were concerned with were spiritual in essence and ethnically identified. They weren't afraid of catching disease — they were afraid of catching culture. Baptism was the cure to exposure. There are several Old Testament passages that refer to the spiritual purification done by washing with water,[78] as well as some New Testament writings that connect water baptism with the Hebrew passage through the Red Sea,[79] although this latter connection appears to exist primarily as a historical example of the former principle.

The problem with defining the practice of baptism with the Essenes is, since there was no unity between the separate communities, there was no standard of practice and, therefore, no singular understanding of it. In other words, it may not be possible to explicitly define this Jewish baptism based on direct evidence. However, we *can* come up with a possible range of understandings

---

[78] Exod 29:4; 30:20–21; Lev 13:1–15:32

[79] 1 Cor 10:1–2; 1 Pet 3:18–22Schlesinger, E. R. (2012, 2013, 2014, 2015). "Sacraments." In J. D. Barry, D. Bomar, D. R. Brown, R. Klippenstein, D. Mangum, C. Sinclair Wolcott, ... W. Widder (Eds.), *The Lexham Bible Dictionary*. Bellingham, WA: Lexham Press.

based upon the problems they faced and how baptism may functionally provide a solution to those problems.

The main problem is easy to identify. It is the Roman occupation of Israel. It was probably the biggest reason that the Essenes left their homes in the cities and villages and fled into the wilderness. This was the problem of direct exposure to gentile influence and could be eliminated or reduced by avoiding anything connected with gentile culture.

The secondary problem was indirect exposure, or exposure that happened without their direct intention. It could also be exposure that occurred without their knowledge or in situations they could not avoid. Both of these kinds of exposure were specifically tied to gentile culture, but they were also connected to things considered spiritually unclean that were not unique to a specific culture. Death and disease are examples of this that the Jews had to deal with even before they were taken over by foreign nations.

The Jewish response to this second kind of exposure was the ritual sacrifices made in the Temple. Those sacrifices spiritually purified the one making the offering and symbolically "washed them clean." However, the Essenes were faced with a problem. When the Romans took over Jerusalem and the priests began compromising the Jewish faith, the choice to leave to live in the wilderness created the consequence of eliminating access to the Temple and, with it, the ability of being cleansed from that indirect or unintended exposure to unclean things.

How then did baptism go from a ceremonial washing of hands and feet for the priests or a cleansing practice for those suffering from disease to something that related to spiritual consecration and perhaps deliverance? It grew from those practices because the Essenes did not have access to the Temple and needed a new way to handle spiritual uncleanness.

The public effect of this baptism, therefore, was an initiation (and perhaps a maintenance) of a person into a sub-category of Jews who believed that the Jewish people as a whole were no longer *set apart* as the people of God and they were gathering a community of the few faithful or *remnant*, of which the Old Testament prophets spoke.[80] They were being set apart, not just from the gentiles, but also from the other Jews whom they saw as being corrupted by gentile influence.

The Wilderness vs. the World

A line in the sand

The Essenes drew a line in the sand that marked the difference between the righteous and the unrighteous, the elect and those destined to perish by God's coming judgment. This is evident from their physical departure from civilization into the wilderness, their disassociation with those who were not of their community, their frequent cleansing rituals, and their strict lifestyles. It took much more than simply getting wet to join their community. We see that in John the Baptist's own preaching:

> *He said therefore to the crowds that came out to be baptized by him, "You brood of vipers! Who warned you to flee from the wrath to come? Bear fruits in keeping with repentance. And do not begin to say to yourselves, 'We have Abraham as our father.' For I tell you, God is able from these stones to raise up children for Abraham. Even now the axe is laid to the root of the trees. Every tree therefore that does not bear good fruit is cut down and thrown into the fire."*
>
> *And the crowds asked him, "What then shall we do?" And he answered them, "Whoever has two tunics is to share with him who has none, and whoever has food is to do likewise." Tax collectors also came to be baptized and said to him, "Teacher, what shall we do?" And he said to them, "Collect no more than you are authorized to do." Soldiers also asked him, "And we, what shall we do?" And he said to them, "Do not extort money from anyone by threats or by false accusation, and be content with your wages.[81]"*

Bear in mind that John the Baptist was probably not the leader of

---

[80] Examples: Isaiah 10, 11, and 46.

[81] *The Holy Bible: English Standard Version.* (2001). (Lk 3:7–14). Wheaton: Standard Bible Society.

the Essenes, but represented more of the liberal end of their community. He was actually out engaging the public, talking with the other religious leaders as well as "sinful" tax collectors and those who had worked for the Romans. The vast majority of the Essenes just stayed away altogether, which may be why they are not identified in the gospels. The early Christians who wrote the gospels had no real memory of them.

The Essenes were polar opposites of the Sadducees in many ways. They removed themselves from the cities, from political power, from wealth, and from anything that might compromise their spirituality or keep them from being in tune with God. They refused to compromise, and they were willing to let the rest of the Jews be lost. They had a very high respect for the Law of Moses, as did the Pharisees, but I think they had a better understanding of the spirit of the law as opposed to just the letter of the Law. They were focused as much or more on the ancient prophets who taught about a day of judgment and the coming Messiah who would lead it.

Unlike the Sadducees, who believed God had left them on their own, or the Zealots and Pharisees, who believed they had a particular role in helping bring that day of judgment about, the Essenes believed that it was entirely in God's hands. For some, it may have been a belief in the miraculous power of God that needed no human help. For others, though, I suspect they may have taken the cynical position of Jonah, who simply sat back outside of town in hopes of watching the fireworks as God prepared to judge Ninevah.[82] Either way, these communities and the individuals in them took on a prophetic role, speaking truth not just in words but in the way they lived their lives. It was this authentic prophetic voice, lived out in the flesh, that drew the crowds into the wilderness to be baptized in the Jordan River and would later be drawn out to follow Jesus Himself, forsaking businesses, families, and the comforts of home to embrace a new lifestyle following God.

The Prophet

We need to return for just a moment to the history of ancient Israel. From the time of Moses through the time of King David, the

---

[82] See Jonah 3.

prophet was given a special place of honor either as *the* leader of the people, or the one who chose on behalf of God and anointed the ruler. He or she was the Ambassador from Heaven sent to make sure the rulers and the people of this earthly colony were behaving themselves.

After the time of Solomon, though, that earthly colony revolted, and the ambassadors were no longer treated with such distinction. Their jobs did not end, but the perks that had gone with them did. Many were mocked, imprisoned, tortured, and killed by the very nations they were trying to serve, particularly during the reign of some of the unfaithful kings of Israel and Judah. Their mission did not change — they were still the ambassadors from God to Israel, but their context was not the same.

No longer did they keep counsel to the king; they found themselves instead speaking truth to an abusive and abused political power. They cried out from the dungeons they sat in or the wells they were lowered into and demanded justice for the poor and oppressed and repentance from the idolatry that so often entangled the politics and culture of Israel. On behalf of God, they issued a call out to Israel — a call to return to God.

This call invited a response from Israel. All too often that invitation to respond was ignored or returned with violence toward the prophet. Ironically, Jonah was one of the most successful prophets in terms of getting a positive response of repentance from his hearers, yet he was perhaps the prophet who cared the least for the people to which God sent him.[83] Meanwhile, Jeremiah was mistreated by the people of Judah whom he cared for so much and got nowhere near the response from them that Jonah got from Ninevah.[84]

The role of prophet is a role created by God, not only to speak truth in words, but to live that truth by example. It is a role that exemplifies the spiritual connection with God that the Essenes sought as well as the presence in the world that the Sadducees desired. In the first

---

[83] See Jonah 1
[84] See Jeremiah 15:10

century, there was a need for the prophet to remind God's people that there was a spiritual battle taking place and that God was fighting on their side, whether they could see Him or not. God wanted to open their eyes to the spiritual reality around them and He wanted them to respond by turning away from the things holding them back and holding them down.

That is the call that John's gospel gave to the people of the first century. Come out of the dark and walk with God in the light.

The Response

The Incarnation: The Word Made Flesh

John is unique in his approach to writing about Jesus. While Matthew, Mark, and Luke take some differing approaches to telling the story of the life, ministry, death, and resurrection of Jesus — each emphasizing different aspects of that story — John seems to have thrown out the script and started from the drawing board when writing his gospel. He literally goes back to the beginning... the very beginning:

> *In the beginning was the Word, and the Word was with God, and the Word was God. He was in the beginning with God. All things were made through him, and without him was not anything made that was made. In him was life, and the life was the light of men. The light shines in the darkness, and the darkness has not overcome it.*[85]

In five short verses, John inserts the story of Jesus into a much greater story about the creation of everything and introduces the "Word" as the primary agent of this story. He also introduces this narrative of the light and dark in conflict, but sets it up in such a way that this conflict is not matched evenly on both sides. The light, he writes, shines in the darkness (present tense) and the darkness has not overcome it. Even if a future victory for the light is only implied, he clearly sets up a precedent that the light has gone through the entire history of creation undefeated in its battles with the darkness.

---

[85] *The Holy Bible: English Standard Version.* (2001). (Jn 1:1–5). Wheaton: Standard Bible Society.

John the Baptist is a witness to that light, and particularly in the opening story of the baptism of Jesus. This "Word," this light, this God enters our world and becomes flesh, but the conflict is not only with the darkness, but also with the people of the world, who did not recognize or follow Him.

> *And the Word became flesh and dwelt among us, and we have seen his glory, glory as of the only Son from the Father, full of grace and truth. (John bore witness about him, and cried out, "This was he of whom I said, 'He who comes after me ranks before me, because he was before me.'") For from his fullness we have all received, grace upon grace. For the law was given through Moses; grace and truth came through Jesus Christ. No one has ever seen God; the only God, who is at the Father's side, he has made him known.*[86]

John sets up this entire gospel message by describing Jesus as the *incarnation* of God. This means that Jesus is God in-the-flesh. Incarnation is a term usually left to the disciplines of theology and philosophy, which is a shame because it is one of the most important parts of any practical spirituality. It has ethical implications. It has aesthetic applications, and it has political applications.

The very existence of the Incarnation shapes our ethics by showing us that human flesh does not overpower the Spirit of God. Whereas Matthew's gospel *tells* us to "be perfect as your heavenly Father is perfect,"[87] John *shows* us what that perfection looks like when it is lived by a human being. Does that mean Matthew does not believe in the Incarnation? No. It is simply a matter of emphasis here. Matthew leads with the genealogy of Abraham to Jesus to show His connection to the line of David. John chooses to lead with the incarnation instead.

There are aesthetic applications when you realize that holiness and goodness can indeed exist in this world and while God may not be depicted in a dead image, God can apparently be depicted in human life. That in itself changes what we consider true beauty to be.

---

[86] *The Holy Bible: English Standard Version.* (2001). (Jn 1:14–18). Wheaton: Standard Bible Society.
[87] Matthew 5:43

Along those aesthetic lines, John shows us the incarnation and what that means for us politically. Here is Jesus, ambassador from heaven — not as the prophets, who are from our world — representing God, but someone from God coming to represent God to us, and ultimately to represent us to Him. In our political areas, we have ambassadors who leave their home country and live in a foreign land in order to influence politics and represent their home country before the other nations. It is a task that maintains a relationship between the nations, and this relationship between two groups of people is made manifest in the ambassadors themselves.

Since this is such a critical relationship, the person chosen for this job is usually a person very well respected by both nations. However, this also means the ambassador cannot be in their home country maintaining leadership there; this person must be in the foreign country. It can become quite a dangerous position if the relationship between the nations goes poorly. Therefore, ambassadors are usually people who are respected, but not *essential* to their home country.

God had used prophets in the past as His ambassadors to Israel, but now there is a new kind of ambassador:

> And he began to speak to them in parables. "A man planted a vineyard and put a fence around it and dug a pit for the winepress and built a tower, and leased it to tenants and went into another country. When the season came, he sent a servant to the tenants to get from them some of the fruit of the vineyard. And they took him and beat him and sent him away empty-handed. Again he sent to them another servant, and they struck him on the head and treated him shamefully. And he sent another, and him they killed. And so with many others: some they beat, and some they killed. He had still one other, a beloved son. Finally he sent him to them, saying, 'They will respect my son.' But those tenants said to one another, 'This is the heir. Come, let us kill him, and the inheritance will be ours.' And they took him and killed him and threw him out of the vineyard. What will the owner of the vineyard do? He will come and destroy the tenants and give the vineyard to others. Have you not read this Scripture:
>
>> "'The stone that the builders rejected
>> has become the cornerstone;
>> this was the Lord's doing,

and it is marvelous in our eyes'?"

And they were seeking to arrest him but feared the people, for they perceived that he had told the parable against them. So they left him and went away.[88]

The Kingdom of Heaven did not only send a respected and essential person into the world as an ambassador. God sent the *most* respected and *most* essential person to be His ambassador — His only Son and heir to the Kingdom of Heaven. This is part of the message of all the gospels — the person God sent from Heaven is His own Son!

John expands on that premise though by showing how very connected God the Father and Jesus, His Son are throughout the entire gospel. For John, Incarnation does not simply mean that the closest family resemblance is here. According to John, Jesus is God Himself, in the flesh.

7 Miracles

Jesus performed many miracles according to the gospels and Matthew, Mark, and Luke treat the recording in order of their occurrence (loosely) and often organized by subject. For instance, they all start with the casting out of demons and healing miracles before they get to stories of raising the dead, feeding the 5,000 people, and walking on water. The miracles act as a sort of narrative buildup that is culminated in the resurrection of Jesus Himself and His final ascension to Heaven.

John has a different perspective when it comes to miracles. He builds the first half of his gospel around seven specific miracles. Each of these miracles is used to show something about Jesus and tie the ministry of Jesus back into this concept of Incarnation. He handpicks them, with less concern for the chronology or their amount of effect and more concern with what they say about who Jesus is. These miracles are: water into wine,[89] healing the official's

---

[88] *The Holy Bible: English Standard Version.* (2001). (Mk 12:1–12). Wheaton: Standard Bible Society.
[89] John 2:1-11

son,[90] healing at the pool of Bethesda,[91] feeding the five thousand,[92] walking on water,[93] healing the man born blind,[94] and raising Lazarus from the dead.[95] These miracles play an integral part of who Jesus is, and it is important that we understand them spiritually so that we can understand their political ramifications.

Miracle 1: Water into Wine

The first miracle in John's gospel has always been a bit mysterious to me. Alcohol in and of itself has political influence, economic influence, psychological influence, and sometimes even spiritual influence in our lives. When alcohol is mentioned, particularly in many societies today, it is difficult to parse through the lens of our current context and return to a time where it, frankly, was not such a big deal.

For example, deaths due to intoxication while driving did not occur in Jesus's day. There were no motorized vehicles, and most people just walked from place to place. The alcohol made was not as strong nor did it come in as many varieties as we have today. While it certainly still had some addictive properties to it, it was simply not as available to the common person as it is today. It was essentially a luxury item.

That is important to understand in this passage. Jesus is not setting up a brewery or distillery here. He is providing a luxury item for a wedding celebration that, while it was a common experience, it was not an everyday experience. It was probably not even a monthly experience. There is an incredible articulation of balance here as John unashamedly describes this story of Jesus using miraculous power to transform water into wine:

> *On the third day there was a wedding at Cana in Galilee, and the mother of Jesus was there. Jesus also was invited to the wedding with his disciples. When the wine ran out, the mother of Jesus said to him,*

---

[90] John 4:43-54
[91] John 5:1-9
[92] John 6:1-5
[93] John 6:16-25
[94] John 9:1-41
[95] John 11:1-44

"They have no wine." And Jesus said to her, "Woman, what does this have to do with me? My hour has not yet come." His mother said to the servants, "Do whatever he tells you.[96] "

The miracles begin with Jesus (and his disciples) at a wedding celebrating with his mother. I fully expect they were drinking — not because John says so anywhere, but, as stated above, alcohol simply was not the social issue then that it is today. More importantly, hospitality was a major issue. To refuse the hospitality of the host, regardless of personal issues was a major social insult in this society that had no concept of diets, allergies, or personal preferences regarding food and drink. In the ancient Middle East, up through the Roman occupation, you were simply grateful to be offered anything, and, in a Jewish household, to a Jew, nothing would have been suspect. Furthermore, Jesus is accused by the Pharisees as being one who hangs out with drunks throughout His ministry, so there is no reason to claim this as the one time Jesus celebrated with alcohol.[97]

Even so, Jesus does not initiate this miracle nor draw undue attention to Himself by it. It almost makes me wonder if Jesus had to pick seven miracles to record, if this one would have even been considered, let alone included as the first. His own statement comes as the question to which all the miracles stand as a testimony: "*What does this have to do with me?*" That is the question we all must find an answer to if we are to understand this miracle. He knew His time of drawing the attention of the whole Middle Eastern world had not yet arrived, so He kept this particular miracle as quiet as possible.

Now there were six stone water jars there for the Jewish rites of purification, each holding twenty or thirty gallons. Jesus said to the servants, "Fill the jars with water." And they filled them up to the brim. And he said to them, "Now draw some out and take it to the

---

[96] *The Holy Bible: English Standard Version.* (2001). (Jn 2:1–5). Wheaton: Standard Bible Society.

[97] For John came neither eating nor drinking, and they say, 'He has a demon.' The Son of Man came eating and drinking, and they say, 'Look at him! A glutton and a drunkard, a friend of tax collectors and sinners!' Yet wisdom is justified by her deeds." *The Holy Bible: English Standard Version.* (2001). (Mt 11:18–19). Wheaton: Standard Bible Society.

master of the feast." So they took it. When the master of the feast tasted the water now become wine, and did not know where it came from (though the servants who had drawn the water knew), the master of the feast called the bridegroom and said to him, "Everyone serves the good wine first, and when people have drunk freely, then the poor wine. But you have kept the good wine until now.[98]"

Six stone jars were set aside for the ritual purification by washing. This ritual washing is very closely tied to the ritual baths practiced by the Essenes and the baptisms done in the Jordan River, so these jars tell us two things about this household. First, this is a Jewish household that is trying to maintain a level of spiritual purity (perhaps inspired by the nearness of the Passover celebration). On the other hand, though, ritual washing was supposed to be done by "living" or running water, not to be stored in jars. While this water was probably not especially dirty water, it was not drinking water, nor was it even truly appropriate for the use of ritual washing.[99]

The transformation of this substandard water, in substandard vessels, and its transformation into wine — a luxury item of celebration — makes a significant spiritual statement. The concern and practice for ritual purity is at once exceeded and redirected to celebration. It is like a sneak preview of the ministry of Christ that is to come. Yes, baptism is a wonderful thing, but it is just the beginning. For these Jews, who were so concerned with being ritually cleansed, particularly for the holy celebrations, Jesus invites them to take in and drink the very water that was meant to cleanse the inside. As far as I am aware, it is an unspoken rule that you do not drink the baptism water. You certainly do not serve it at a party. Yet that was precisely what Jesus was asking this servant to do.

When it was dipped out though, it was not water, pure or otherwise, it was wine... and not just any wine. The master of the feast proclaimed it as the good wine, or the wine that was to be served first while the guests still cared about taste. John takes the ritual of purification and turns it into a joyful celebration. Even more, Scott

---

[98] *The Holy Bible: English Standard Version.* (2001). (Jn 2:6–10). Wheaton: Standard Bible Society.
[99] Keener, C. S. (2012). *The Gospel of John: A Commentary & 2* (Vol. 1, p. 510). Grand Rapids, MI: Baker Academic.

McKnight points out that the sheer abundance of wine here is overwhelming. For this wedding party, Jesus creates roughly 180 gallons — over 900 bottles of wine.[100]

The idea of political purification today is ripe with racial, ethnic, and cultural sentiments that all too often lead to hatred, violence, and suffering on a mass scale. This miracle did not mark a line drawn in the sand between those who were friends and enemies of God. Quite the opposite. It marked a union of two becoming one, and on that day, in that celebration, the very ritual tools made to separate became instruments to celebrate a union. Put another way, Jesus used the concept of baptism (setting apart) to celebrate a marriage (coming together) in one move.

What are the instruments of our political separation? We have colors and mascots that represent political parties, whose existence may be the greatest instruments of separation we have. In many cases, when asked about my political beliefs, I am not asked about particular issues. I am simply asked which party I support. How can Christ take these instruments of separation and transform them into a celebration of union?

Miracle 2: Healing the Official's Son

> *After the two days he departed for Galilee. (For Jesus himself had testified that a prophet has no honor in his own hometown.) So when he came to Galilee, the Galileans welcomed him, having seen all that he had done in Jerusalem at the feast. For they too had gone to the feast.*

> *So he came again to Cana in Galilee, where he had made the water wine. And at Capernaum there was an official whose son was ill. When this man heard that Jesus had come from Judea to Galilee, he went to him and asked him to come down and heal his son, for he was at the point of death. So Jesus said to him, "Unless you see signs and wonders you will not believe." The official said to him, "Sir, come down before my child dies." Jesus said to him, "Go; your son will live." The man believed the word that Jesus spoke to him and went on his way.*

---

[100] McKnight, 2014, p. 148

As he was going down, his servants met him and told him that his son was recovering. So he asked them the hour when he began to get better, and they said to him, "Yesterday at the seventh hour the fever left him." The father knew that was the hour when Jesus had said to him, "Your son will live." And he himself believed, and all his household. This was now the second sign that Jesus did when he had come from Judea to Galilee.[101]

This is a story about faith. Here again, Jesus returned to Cana of Galilee and found more welcome there in a place that had more gentile influence than in His own more Jewish hometown of Nazareth. An official from the nearby town of Capernaum came to see if Jesus would come back with him and heal his son who was at the point of death. Jesus told the official that he would not believe unless this miracle was accompanied by signs and wonders, but the official persisted. Jesus then turned and announced that the boy would live. When the man returned home, he found that this was true and that the boy's fever had left him at the time Jesus announced that he would live.

It is a story of faith, not because anyone does anything that demonstrates great faith, but because it is faith shown in the lack of signs and wonders, yet it yields the same results. Everyone takes a back seat in this story besides Jesus and this father. With only the power of His word, Jesus changes the outcome and heals this boy who is miles away. There is no laying on of hands or chanting. He simply says it is and it is. It is not noted whether this man is Jewish or gentile, which tells us that it doesn't matter who you are. What matters in this story is this: In the face of insurmountable odds, will we seek Jesus — and when we do not get a show of divine intervention, will we continue along our way in faith that what He says, goes?

It strikes me as ironic that politics are built upon and held together by promises kept in faith. We make promises to our leaders and they make promises to us, and we trust they will fulfill them and that we will fulfill ours. Yet our politics today are not marked by faith, but by doubt. It has been almost 40 years since Watergate, and we have

---

[101] *The Holy Bible: English Standard Version.* (2001). (Jn 4:43–54). Wheaton: Standard Bible Society.

lived through an entire generation, of presidents and national leaders who were not trusted. Distrust in the government has become the new norm and there has been an entire generation raised that has never known otherwise. It has followed a similar shift in distrust in God. We campaign on distrust now, not stating what we stand for, but spending our energy and resources attacking our opponents. This tactic is not new, but neither does it work well in the long run. We have changed the environment, changed the rules of the game so that political winners fall faster than ever from the returning waves of distrust that carried them into power.

This miracle shows us that faith in anything begins with a faith in God, even when we do not understand — perhaps especially when we do not understand. Facing an environment hostile to anything related to trust, it shows that it only takes one to change the rules again — particularly when that faith is placed in God. Will we believe God even if we cannot see the proof before us? Can we trust God to be God, not just in the spiritual world, but in the brokenness of our political situations, or will we take matters into our own hands?

Miracle 3: Healing at the Pool of Bethesda

> *After this there was a feast of the Jews, and Jesus went up to Jerusalem.*
>
> *Now there is in Jerusalem by the Sheep Gate a pool, in Aramaic called Bethesda, which has five roofed colonnades. In these lay a multitude of invalids — blind, lame, and paralyzed. One man was there who had been an invalid for thirty-eight years. When Jesus saw him lying there and knew that he had already been there a long time, he said to him, "Do you want to be healed?" The sick man answered him, "Sir, I have no one to put me into the pool when the water is stirred up, and while I am going another steps down before me." Jesus said to him, "Get up, take up your bed, and walk." And at once the man was healed, and he took up his bed and walked.[102]*

This second healing miracle does not have the obstacle of distance. It showcases the power of Jesus over time. Here in this place of

---

[102] *The Holy Bible: English Standard Version.* (2001). (Jn 5:1–9). Wheaton: Standard Bible Society.

physical debilitation, surrounded by dozens, maybe more than a hundred blind, sick, and lame people, Jesus picks out one and asks him an audacious question. *"Do you want to be healed?"* The question is so direct and the answer so obvious that it almost invites sarcasm. It is like asking that question to someone lying in a hospital room.

Except, that is not quite true. A better analogy would be that it is like someone who has lain in a hospital bed for 38 years. Would they still want to be healed? Maybe not. Maybe in that amount of time they would have given up hope and just wished for death. Maybe they had grown so used to the injury that they did not even realize they were hurt. Maybe this man showed up at this pool each day, not because he expected to be healed, but because this was his community — these were the type of people he could understand.

It was in the middle of this hurt community that Jesus called him out and asked him if he wanted out. *"No one will help me. They all rush to get in front of me whenever I get a chance to get out."* Jesus called to him and he responded with excuses. True though they may be, he did not really answer the question Jesus asked. He did not listen to what was asked; he answered a different question instead. He answered the question, *"Why have you not healed yourself?"* But that is not what he was asked. Jesus only wanted to know if he still wanted to be healed.

Time does strange things to us. Some things heal. Other things get infected. Most things scar over as a reminder of the wound. It happens in individuals and it happens in communities as well. It affects our political perspectives. When we are at a place that holds history, good and especially bad, we get defensive. We place memorials at the roadsides where loved ones have been killed. We retell ourselves those stories in our minds over and over again.

Our perspectives change, though, and the details come in and out of focus until they fit whatever grand design we are trying to justify for ourselves and others. It is our way of making sense of why bad things happen to us, and we all do it. Jesus calls us out of that, though. Instead of asking for a reason we are the way we are, He simply asks if we want to be healed.

How often have we been hurt in the political and community battles we face and find there is no way past the hurt, past the wounds. Generations upon generations compound scars upon scars until no one remembers what started the war, only that we were born either to cut or to bleed. It is in the midst of those situations that Jesus calls us out and asks us if *we* want to be healed. Again, He gives us no flashy show of power. He only asks us to start living like we are healed, picking up our bed, and walking into something new.

Miracle 4: Feeding of the 5,000

> *After this Jesus went away to the other side of the Sea of Galilee, which is the Sea of Tiberias. And a large crowd was following him, because they saw the signs that he was doing on the sick. Jesus went up on the mountain, and there he sat down with his disciples. Now the Passover, the feast of the Jews, was at hand. Lifting up his eyes, then, and seeing that a large crowd was coming toward him, Jesus said to Philip, "Where are we to buy bread, so that these people may eat?" He said this to test him, for he himself knew what he would do. Philip answered him, "Two hundred denarii worth of bread would not be enough for each of them to get a little." One of his disciples, Andrew, Simon Peter's brother, said to him, "There is a boy here who has five barley loaves and two fish, but what are they for so many?" Jesus said, "Have the people sit down." Now there was much grass in the place. So the men sat down, about five thousand in number. Jesus then took the loaves, and when he had given thanks, he distributed them to those who were seated. So also the fish, as much as they wanted. And when they had eaten their fill, he told his disciples, "Gather up the leftover fragments, that nothing may be lost." So they gathered them up and filled twelve baskets with fragments from the five barley loaves left by those who had eaten. When the people saw the sign that he had done, they said, "This is indeed the Prophet who is to come into the world!*[103]*"*

The fourth miracle recorded by John is the first miracle shared by all the gospel writers.[104] In this story, Jesus performs a miracle of provision when the number of people following Jesus was so great but the food was scarce. For people in the wilderness of first century

---

[103] *The Holy Bible: English Standard Version.* (2001). (Jn 6:1–14). Wheaton: Standard Bible Society.
[104] See also, Matthew 14, Mark 6, and Luke 9.

Palestine, this would have been a major problem. Not only were there no stores to buy food, but even hunting and scavenging would not have turned up enough food to feed that many people.

As opposed to the previous two medical-related miracles performed, this is an economic miracle. The demand vastly outweighed the supply. Can you imagine what would have happened without the leadership of Jesus? "There is a boy with five barley loaves and two fish," says Andrew. Panic sets in. Someone from the crowd yells, "Let's get him." They leap upon him while one woman quickly makes off with one of the loaves of bread. The story ends with a man choking to death on fish bones having tried to gorge himself on it before anyone else could take it from him. This is what is sometimes referred to as "human nature," but I believe is something closer to animalistic behavior than anything uniquely human. It is a mess.

The economies in our lives can drive us into frenzies when they get out of balance. Very little causes as much irrational panic as drastic changes in/to them. Some people pack their bags and run off with anything they can carry, while others turn their homes into fortresses, stocking up on non-perishable goods to wait out a time of trouble. The number of suicides increases, and violence to one another rises as well.

Jesus does not panic, though. He has his disciples help assess the situation and determine the resources at hand. He calms the people and has them sit down. Then he gives thanks to God for the resources they have. As He distributes them, they miraculously feed the entire crowd and afterward there are twelve baskets full... one for each of the disciples.

Jesus demonstrates three important characteristics that I think are often lacking in our economic and political aspects of life. First, He demonstrated a calm, honest assessment. Occasionally I have seen this, but more often we approach our economy with a defensiveness and a desire to blame shortcomings on the opposition. Whether those accusations have any truth in them or not, it never changes the present situation. Secondly, before anyone receives anything, the resources are gathered together and gratitude is given to God. Today was a good day for the stock market, but I did not read anyone giving

God thanks for it among the national press releases. Finally, Jesus and His disciples eat whatever is left. The trend in government has been that the leaders have first pick, and the crowd gets whatever is left, particularly regarding the economy. A nation can be in tremendous debt while its leaders are millionaires. Not so in the Kingdom of God.

Miracle 5: Walking on Water

> *When evening came, his disciples went down to the sea, got into a boat, and started across the sea to Capernaum. It was now dark, and Jesus had not yet come to them. The sea became rough because a strong wind was blowing. When they had rowed about three or four miles, they saw Jesus walking on the sea and coming near the boat, and they were frightened. But he said to them, "It is I; do not be afraid." Then they were glad to take him into the boat, and immediately the boat was at the land to which they were going.*

> *On the next day the crowd that remained on the other side of the sea saw that there had been only one boat there, and that Jesus had not entered the boat with his disciples, but that his disciples had gone away alone. Other boats from Tiberias came near the place where they had eaten the bread after the Lord had given thanks. So when the crowd saw that Jesus was not there, nor his disciples, they themselves got into the boats and went to Capernaum, seeking Jesus.*

> *When they found him on the other side of the sea, they said to him, "Rabbi, when did you come here?"[105]*

We often work ourselves into a frenzy during drastic economic changes. We also panic in times of environmental disaster. Floods, earthquakes, wildfires, and tornadoes cause havoc in communities, and it takes years to recover from them. In our age of information, the panic spreads out even to those who are not directly affected by the events themselves, but who are filled with anxiety, wondering if it will happen to them as well.

---

[105] *The Holy Bible: English Standard Version.* (2001). (Jn 6:16–25). Wheaton: Standard Bible Society.

This miracle of Jesus walking on the water during the storm shows two things about the leadership of Jesus. First, Jesus is not afraid of the storm. He does not wait for the storm to stop, nor does He cause it to stop before going to the disciples. The power He demonstrates is not control over the environment (although there are similar stories that shows He has this power) — He shows control over Himself. While the world is storming all around Him, He remains at peace, and He shares that peace with the disciples with Him. He exercised control of the situation by remaining in control of Himself.

What happened next is even more telling. The crowd, whom Jesus had fed, were looking for Him, presumably to get more food, and did not realize that He had made it to the other side of the sea. He had gone out to be with the disciples in their time of crisis, and He had not told anyone else where He had gone. This reminds me a little of the teaching Jesus gave on giving in the Sermon on the Mount. Give in such a way that even your left hand does not know what your right hand is doing. Don't make a show of it. Here again, we have Jesus, God incarnate, performing miracles and doing it quietly. If anyone could make a show of it, it would be Him, but He keeps choosing a powerful subtlety in His actions.

What difference does it make? Well, consider this from a political perspective. Here is Jesus, leading a staff of twelve men, out making a difference in the lives around them. They build a following, which becomes a crowd of thousands. This crowd is not healing, teaching, or preaching the way the disciples are. They are consumers. They come to be healed or taught, and many of them just come for the food. They draw time and energy away from working with the disciples, and they hold Jesus in one place rather than blessing Him and sending Him on to other areas of Israel that have as many people in need of Him as they. In their own way, they become a storm of people that seeks to keep them all filled with anxiety and stuck in one place, or moving in a direction they are pushing. They are the lobbyists in the life of Jesus.

Being lobbyists does not make them right or wrong. Jesus does not ignore them, nor does He allow Himself to be led by them. He does not put on a show for them and He does not allow Himself to become dependent upon them. He does what is right because it is right, not because of who sees Him. And rather than getting tied up in deals made between Himself and those who get Him into power, He instead chooses to help out of His own generosity, and then move on. Do our politics exemplify that degree of self-control that leads to the freedom to step up and truly lead, especially in times of crisis?

Miracle 6: Healing the Man Born Blind

> *As he passed by, he saw a man blind from birth. And his disciples asked him, "Rabbi, who sinned, this man or his parents, that he was born blind?" Jesus answered, "It was not that this man sinned, or his parents, but that the works of God might be displayed in him. We must work the works of him who sent me while it is day; night is coming, when no one can work. As long as I am in the world, I am the light of the world." Having said these things, he spit on the ground and made mud with the saliva. Then he anointed the man's eyes with the mud and said to him, "Go, wash in the pool of Siloam" (which means Sent). So he went and washed and came back seeing.[106]*

Here is another healing miracle and one that gained Jesus notoriety throughout Judea. There were probably many blind people healed by Jesus, and blindness itself is not necessarily worse than paralysis, leprosy, or any other malady that Jesus healed. It was unique in its own challenges. A paralyzed or weakened person may not be able to move around well, but at least they could see to be aware of trouble coming toward them. Blindness was a challenge that made a person perpetually vulnerable to the things they could not see coming.

The two particular qualities that draw the attention of this blind man are the concepts of sin and birth. The prevailing concept of sickness, disease, and other physical defects that occurred outside of direct injury were almost always linked to sin. There was a widespread karma-like notion that good things happened to good people and bad things happened to bad people. This is a very basic superstition that is present in a multitude of cultures and remains with us today. This man becomes a case study for the spiritual relationship between

---

[106] *The Holy Bible: English Standard Version.* (2001). (Jn 9:1–7). Wheaton: Standard Bible Society.

sin and sickness.

One of the reasons this man is spotlighted as a case study is because he did not become blind later in life, but had been born blind. This drew even more speculation about sin. Even if infants were judged for their actions, a newborn may not have had enough time to do anything bad enough to warrant a punishment such as blindness. Therefore, this man's parents — a third party — is brought into the equation and the disciples approach Jesus with the question: "Rabbi, who sinned, this man or his parents, that he was born blind?"

Do you hear the emphasis of the question? They already assumed that sin was the cause of this blindness. Their superstition came out immediately, but they did not know whom to blame. (The most important question when dealing with superstition.) Jesus answered directly that no one was to blame. This suffering was not brought on by anyone's wrongdoing. Instead it was done to create an opportunity for the work of God to be displayed.

As everyone stands around and tries to figure out what in the world Jesus means that this suffering was not caused by sin, Jesus proclaims that He is the Light of the World, and that while He is there, He will work. He spits on the ground, rubs the mud created there on the man's eyes, and tells him to go wash it off in the pool of Siloam. The man obeys and, when he returns, he is able to see for the first time in his life.

Suffering brings out our superstition, and superstition puts us on the defensive. If we can explain what we do not understand, we may be able to control the situation and protect ourselves from the suffering we see around us. I believe it is why we are all so quick to place blame. If we can find the fault, we do not have to fear. It is the most unsettling idea that your health or your life could be taken from you at any moment, and there is nothing you can do about it. Yet this terrifying thought may be closer to the truth than we can handle. Ecclesiastes, a book of wisdom in the Old Testament, ends with this passage:

> The end of the matter; all has been heard. Fear God and keep his commandments, for this is the whole duty of man. For God will bring

every deed into judgment, with every secret thing, whether good or evil.[107]

The Book of Proverbs from the Old Testament begins with the statement that wisdom begins with the Fear of the Lord, just as Ecclesiastes ends. So these two books of wisdom literature in scripture are bookended by the idea that understanding is centered around the fear of God. If we include the book of Job, we have a narrative account of that concept: The idea that suffering happens to both the good and the bad, that it is not dealt out according to amount of sin, and that God finds ways to glorify Himself *in the midst* of suffering.

This blind man was later interrogated by the Jewish leaders, along with his parents, to find out exactly what Jesus had done. It is one thing to restore someone to the normal health they enjoy. It was another to improve upon the health they had been given at birth. This level of healing crossed over into improving upon the creation of God. It was incredibly disturbing to the Jewish leaders that someone would not only claim to have the power of God, but actually be able to use it.

What are the political implications of this case of sin and sickness? What are the applications of Jesus refusing to play the blame game? Christ calls us to give up laying blame for suffering and instead to work to bring healing. Places of suffering are not to be used as opportunities to criticize our opponents or any others, but instead opportunities to see God at work around us.

What does it mean to see God at work in politics? The legitimacy of this question may say more about the state of our political affairs and the lack of faithfulness to God that exists there than we are comfortable. Yet I think that makes the question all the more important. When and where have you seen God at work in our politics? As Jesus pointed out to His disciples, God takes those opportunities to be the Light of the World even when we miss them by not paying attention to Him, or by simply not caring. If He is at work in our politics and we do not see Him, what have we been doing?

---

[107] *The Holy Bible: English Standard Version.* (2001). (Ec 12:13–14). Wheaton: Standard Bible Society.

Miracle 7: Raising Lazarus from the Dead

Then Jesus, deeply moved again, came to the tomb. It was a cave, and a stone lay against it. Jesus said, "Take away the stone." Martha, the sister of the dead man, said to him, "Lord, by this time there will be an odor, for he has been dead four days." Jesus said to her, "Did I not tell you that if you believed you would see the glory of God?" So they took away the stone. And Jesus lifted up his eyes and said, "Father, I thank you that you have heard me. I knew that you always hear me, but I said this on account of the people standing around, that they may believe that you sent me." When he had said these things, he cried out with a loud voice, "Lazarus, come out." The man who had died came out, his hands and feet bound with linen strips, and his face wrapped with a cloth. Jesus said to them, "Unbind him, and let him go.[108]"

The last enemy to be destroyed is death.[109]

I think one of the most important parts of this final miracle was that it did not have to be this way. Jesus had cured sickness and injury, both recent and those that people had dealt with for years. He had cured birth defects. He had cured incurable diseases. He had made small resources feed the multitude and had leftovers. He had stepped across the sea in the middle of a storm. There was nothing He could not do.

Jesus had plenty of advance notice about His friend Lazarus being ill. He could have made it in time, and His disciples told Him so. No, here was a moment that Jesus chose to show up too late. Nearly any other person with the healing powers of Jesus would have stopped what they were doing to go save their friend, and would have made this a completely different story. Jesus, however, was adamant that His agenda was not driven by His personal desires and needs, but simply following where He saw God already at work.[110]

---

[108] *The Holy Bible: English Standard Version.* (2001). (Jn 11:38–44). Wheaton: Standard Bible Society.

[109] *The Holy Bible: English Standard Version.* (2001). (1 Co 15:26). Wheaton: Standard Bible Society.

[110] So Jesus said to them, "Truly, truly, I say to you, the Son can do nothing of his own accord, but only what he sees the Father doing. For whatever the Father does, that the Son does likewise. For the Father loves the Son and shows him all

Jesus let Lazarus die. He waited until he was already buried before He came to visit. Jesus let the friends and family mourn. He waited until every last hope was spent... every last hope except one: Hope in Him.

I think we all believe in a point called "too far gone." It is a point in the life of anything when so much destruction and devastation has occurred physically, mentally, emotionally, and spiritually that we believe the better course is for it to die. As it goes for people, we almost all reach that place by the time we put them in the ground. Yes, we believe that Jesus could bring them back — resuscitate them, but what kind of *quality* of life would they have at that point? When you've lost all sensation in your body, when you've lost multiple limbs, when everything hurts all the time — what kind of life is that and is it even worth living? Death is our enemy throughout our entire life, until at last it becomes our dearest friend.

Jesus took the family of Lazarus through all that suffering, into the experience of death, and then, as they were trying to close the book and move on with life, He showed up and took them back to the tomb. He went to *unfinish* the work that death had finished with Lazarus.

There is an incredible message of hope here. The hope that Christ represents: the hope that Christ Himself *is*, goes far beyond the end of our sight. The point where we give up is the point where He is just getting started. There is nothing He cannot do, or undo. He is the master of life and death and can draw us back simply by calling out to us. What will our response be?

That call goes right to our belief about death. Jesus wanted to demonstrate the power of God that does not fear death. He does not hurry to prevent the end of life, because He knows that life can be given again. He does not worry about the suffering and anguish involved in any death because it is temporary at best. The pain, the hurt, and the loss are real — but they are not forever. This is a call

that he himself is doing. And greater works than these will he show him, so that you may marvel. For as the Father raises the dead and gives them life, so also the Son gives life to whom he will. *The Holy Bible: English Standard Version.* (2001). (Jn 5:19–21). Wheaton: Standard Bible Society.

to face death fearlessly, knowing that, even there, God's glory still shines. No matter what we go through, God is right there with us.

Where does the fear of death usurp the authority in our politics? When do we rush, for the sake of saving life, as Jesus takes His time, arrives too late, and then brings new life?

In the world...

The Power of the Spirit: John 14-16

Let's return for a moment to the Essenes. They were looking for a place, a sanctuary, where they could live their lives serving God without the pressures and distractions of the Roman Empire. Jesus came into the world and did not seem to have a problem staying connected with God right there among all the cultural chaos around Him. Whether it was a wedding where people were drinking and celebrating, walking among the sick and wounded (and potentially unclean), surrounded by a hungry crowd, or walking across a stormy sea, nothing seemed to pull Him away from His focus on God. Not even the death of a dear friend.

I believe this is because Jesus was God incarnate. Looking back at John's first chapter, I think John believed that as well. Without getting into the exact doctrinal parsing of what it means to be God incarnate, I think we can agree that it is something Jesus experienced in a way we will never understand. To know God, to love and be loved by God is one thing... to *be* God is something else entirely. Some might say that Jesus had it easier than us for that reason, and there may be some truth to that. However, in my thirty-some years of life, I have not faced anything approaching the problems and the suffering that Jesus experienced. The problem with trying to face our troubles with the way Jesus did is that we are not Jesus. That is what I believe chapters 14 through 16 are expressly about. How can we be like Jesus?

The short answer is: with the Holy Spirit.

> "Let not your hearts be troubled. Believe in God; believe also in me.[111]

---

[111] *The Holy Bible: English Standard Version.* (2001). (Jn 14:1). Wheaton: Standard Bible Society.

I imagine the disciples were devastated when the truth began to sink in that Jesus was going to leave them. They had been so busy learning from and ministering with Jesus that the three years they had with Him probably flew by. They were finally seeing the end of their time with Him and that question began to fill their hearts. *How can we continue without you?*

Jesus comforted them with two thoughts. First, He told them that His leaving would be temporary and that He would come again to take them with Him. That is a wonderful consolation but it does not answer the question of how they were to carry on in His absence. He made it clear that He *did* expect them to carry on, doing the same things He had done and more. So Jesus gave them another answer as well.

> *"If you love me, you will keep my commandments. And I will ask the Father, and he will give you another Helper, to be with you forever, even the Spirit of truth, whom the world cannot receive, because it neither sees him nor knows him. You know him, for he dwells with you and will be in you.*[112]

> *"These things I have spoken to you while I am still with you. But the Helper, the Holy Spirit, whom the Father will send in my name, he will teach you all things and bring to your remembrance all that I have said to you.*[113]

He promised the Holy Spirit, the Helper, the Spirit of truth, whom the world would not understand, but they would. They would understand because that Spirit would come to live in them. The Holy Spirit would remind them when they forgot what Jesus had taught them. It would fill in the gaps and be their strength where they were weak.

Abiding and Love

In the next chapter, Jesus tell the disciples they must abide in Him,

---

[112] *The Holy Bible: English Standard Version.* (2001). (Jn 14:15–17). Wheaton: Standard Bible Society.
[113] *The Holy Bible: English Standard Version.* (2001). (Jn 14:25–26). Wheaton: Standard Bible Society.

loving one another, and withstanding the hatred that the world has for them. The order of this is important. It is easy to get prideful and believe that we know how to love just fine without someone standing over our shoulder every moment. That is exactly what we need, though. Once we disconnect ourselves from Jesus, through His Spirit, we cannot do anything, and everything falls apart. When we become disconnected from Jesus, love stops, and hatred steps in to take its place.

Loving others does not always come naturally, and Jesus commanded His followers to love, not as the world loves, but as He loves. He wants us to love incarnationally, and the only way we can do that is if we have His Spirit in us, loving through us. That love is more than simply treating one another better than our normal standards of politeness and respect. It is a witness of the love that God has for everyone around us. When we love others, we are not just showing them how much we love them, we are showing them how much God loves them as well. We certainly cannot do that on our own.

> *"But when the Helper comes, whom I will send to you from the Father, the Spirit of truth, who proceeds from the Father, he will bear witness about me. And you also will bear witness, because you have been with me from the beginning".*[114]

Love is our responsibility. Judging and convicting others of sin is not. In Chapter 16, Jesus told His disciples that the Holy Spirit had the task of convicting the world of sin. How does that happen when the Spirit is in us? Is that any different from us convicting the world ourselves?

> Nevertheless, I tell you the truth: it is to your advantage that I go away, for if I do not go away, the Helper will not come to you. But if I go, I will send him to you. And when he comes, he will convict the world concerning sin and righteousness and judgment: concerning sin, because they do not believe in me; concerning righteousness, because I go to the Father, and you will see me no longer; concerning

---

[114] *The Holy Bible: English Standard Version.* (2001). (Jn 15:26–27). Wheaton: Standard Bible Society.

127

judgment, because the ruler of this world is judged.

> "I still have many things to say to you, but you cannot bear
> them now. When the Spirit of truth comes, he will guide you
> into all the truth, for he will not speak on his own authority,
> but whatever he hears he will speak, and he will declare to
> you the things that are to come. He will glorify me, for he
> will take what is mine and declare it to you. All that the
> Father has is mine; therefore I said that he will take what is
> mine and declare it to you.[115]

Jesus says that the Spirit does not speak on its own authority, so
neither do we. We only share what the Spirit gives us to share. In our
day of extreme inclusion and exclusion, that may sound like splitting
hairs, but that is the truth we are given in scripture. Some take that
to mean the Spirit gives us insight into the secret sins of others.
Others have abused this passage to pursue their own agendas in
God's name. Look at what Jesus describes, though.

The Spirit brings messages of the things that are yet to come. It
glorifies Jesus. It declares the things that belong to Him. These are
quite different from judging and condemning others around us. First
of all, prophecies of the future cannot condemn sin unless we are
held accountable for sins we have not yet committed. Secondly,
dwelling on sin does not glorify Jesus. No, I believe this judgment
comes from the last statement about declaring what belongs to Jesus.
The world around us will be judged, not by pointing out what wicked
deeds they have done. It will be judged when Christ returns for His
own, and so many are left behind because they do not abide in Him.

The Essenes sought a sanctuary away from the world. Jesus taught
and empowered his people to be a sanctuary *for* the world as they
became an incarnation of God by abiding in His Spirit.

Greater Things...

John 17 has often been labeled the "High Priestly Prayer" that Jesus

---

[115] The Holy Bible: English Standard Version. (2001). (Jn 16:7–15). Wheaton:
Standard Bible Society.

prayed before his arrest and execution. In this prayer, He prays for unity between His disciples and God and between all the disciples themselves. He asks God to give them the same love and connection that He enjoys with God.

He also prayed for those of us who would come later. He prayed for those who would be connected because of their belief in the witness of those disciples. It was this unity found in Christ, through His Spirit, that leads me to believe that the Church was and is the answer to this prayer. It is not the buildings or the services, but the community of believers that come from every place imaginable, yet drawn together as one to share what God has declared — that they belong to Jesus. They are the light in the world today, sharing the love that the Holy Spirit has put in their hearts, out of gratitude for the love Christ showed us.

> But now I am coming to you, and these things I speak in the world, that they may have my joy fulfilled in themselves. I have given them your word, and the world has hated them because they are not of the world, just as I am not of the world. I do not ask that you take them out of the world, but that you keep them from the evil one. They are not of the world, just as I am not of the world. Sanctify them in the truth; your word is truth. As you sent me into the world, so I have sent them into the world. And for their sake I consecrate myself, that they also may be sanctified in truth.[116]

Christ came from outside our world and called us to Him. The world responded to His love with hate, although some responded by following Him. Those that followed were set apart, not to leave the world, but to be as Jesus was — in the world, but not of the world. That is our calling today.

Do we seek sanctuaries in our politics? Are we motivated simply by wanting to stay safe and be left alone? Or is there a greater calling for us as we lead and select leaders in our life? I believe Christ calls us to be a witness to God's love in all aspects of our life, including

---

[116] *The Holy Bible: English Standard Version.* (2001). (Jn 17:13–19). Wheaton: Standard Bible Society.

politically. What would our world look like if the leaders of the world sought to abide in and be a witness to the love of Christ?

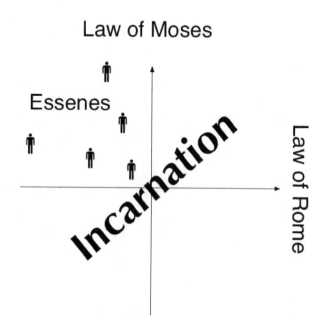

Chapter Seven
Conclusions

The Way, the Life, and the Truth

It is not impossible to be a Christian and a politician. It is not easy though. Politics are a part of life and wherever two or three are gathered together, someone is going to take leadership in one form or another. What makes politics "Christian" is when we remember that when community gathers together in Christ's name, He is there with us.[117]

He is the Way, the Life, and the Truth, and we have seen how He challenged all the Jewish people in their spiritual and political ideas. He challenges us as well. There were four types of Jews in the first century, and there are four types of Christians in our nation today. Those same categories relating to the Law of God and the Law of Man still influence us in tremendous ways.

This comes across in our discussions about the separation or connection between Church and State. These issues are at the root of every faith-related question given to candidates for political office. It is at the heart of every reference to our country (or any other) founded as a "Christian" nation.

The politics inside our churches go round and round, spiraling outward further into extremes with every rotation. They are influenced as much by secular culture around us as either Scripture or the Spirit of God, and we continue to use our reason to justify our experiences rather than to understand them. I believe this is because we do not know the right questions to ask; therefore, we cannot hope to find the answers we need.

There are two questions we need to ask:

---

[117] See Matthew 18:20

1. What are our political values? (Why do we believe what we believe?)

2. How does Jesus engage those values?

While the contexts and some of the specific issues may differ from first century Palestine, the foundations have not. Christian politics will always find itself somewhere on the spectrum of the authority of government and religious institutions. We may claim to follow neither. We may claim to just follow Jesus, but our personal practices will reveal our relationship between the Church and State.

4 Types of Christians

Once you understand your own spiritual and political values, you can find yourself and your faith community on its own chart of Law of God and Law of man. The engagement with the authority of Heaven and the authorities on earth has not changed since the beginning. There are still four types of Jews today and, in addition as God's people, there are four corresponding types of Christians.

There are Christian Pharisees who focus in on following both spiritual and worldly laws as a means of proving their faith and receiving blessing from God. The churches preaching the prosperity gospel — that God will bless you if you just _____ are examples of this. So are the churches who rejoice in salvations but then expect complete life change that is compliant with their understanding of a Christian life, or else they become skeptical as to your salvation. Bear in mind there are aspects of truth in both of these perspectives. These are the churches that believe you cannot be a Christian if you vote for a person or party outside their own parameters. As we have seen in Matthew, Jesus holds us all up to even higher standards than this, but empowers us to get there by His grace. We Christian Pharisees need a greater understanding and experience of spiritual and political grace.

Christian Zealots are rising up more and more, particularly among those who are only marginally involved in the denominational political systems. You may have seen their work on social media but not know their names. A Christian Zealot is one who regularly mixes political and spiritual values, treating them as one under the banner of freedom and often on the premise of "our country was founded upon...". We become Christian Zealots when we push for enforced Christian practices — such as Christian prayer in public schools, led by the administration or teachers. We become Christian Zealots when we want to restrict non-Christians from entering our country. This political persuasion is often seen in political agendas that include freedom to drink, smoke, own and shoot weapons, pray, and preach in whatever manner we please. Mark's gospel demonstrates true freedom comes from submitting ourselves to God's authority and exercising self-control.

On the left are the Christian Sadducees. When we compromise the spiritual values handed down to us (often by Christian Pharisees) and approach the task of interpreting the scriptures with an attitude of: *what is the very least I can do and still be a Christian*, we fall into this Christian Sadducee category. We do this for the sake of mission and sharing the gospel. We do this when we see large groups of people for whom our ministry is not helping. In the United States today, sexuality is one of the subjects we spend lots of time and energy addressing for the sake of including or excluding those whose sexual preferences and practices differ from our own.

Let me use another example that covers a larger group of people. The Fourth Commandment of the Law of Moses is to honor the Sabbath and keep it holy. Yet today, millions of people work on the Sabbath (whether you count it as Saturday or Sunday). Most Americans do not attend church at all, and those who do consider "regular attendance" being once per month. 100 years ago, it was considered a common understanding that if you did not go to church each week, you weren't really a Christian. Certainly, some exceptions were made, but nowhere near the amount of excuses given today. 100 years ago, those who advocated that people could be Christians without attending church services each week would have been considered the extreme liberals and the Christian Sadducees of their day. Times have changed and (to the Christian Pharisees' chagrin) many of those values have been lost for the sake of getting the basic salvation message out to a people who will not accept all the values that have been handed down with our faith.

Luke's gospel directs us to the call of discipleship, preached by Jesus and lived out by the Apostles. He reminds us that our hope is not in ourselves, figuring out a way to keep the gospel going. Our hope is in Christ, through the power of the Holy Spirit, conquering death and being resurrected to a new life we could not salvage ourselves.

Lastly, there are Christian Essenes — groups who have been fed up with the temptations and evils that surround politics and choose to live with as little political interaction as possible. They have had many names through the centuries — from the Desert Fathers, a monastic group who spent time in solitude in the wilderness, to the Anabaptist church of the reformation period, and all the branches that stem reach to those who do not vote and sometimes refuse political citizenship in the places in which they live.

John's gospel reminds us that we are called to be in the world, but not of the world. We are not supposed to escape the world, but be an incarnational message of love and hope so that the world might not perish, but that it would be saved by Christ working through us. We are not called to hide and wait for Jesus — we have a mission, ministry to do, and, as Jesus reminded Peter, "If you love me, feed my sheep."[118]

We have seen how Jesus interacted with those four types of Jews. We have read Scriptures that engage those underlying values and challenge them to a higher standard. Now we take a brief look at how that higher standard, for each set of values, has been modeled throughout the history of politics in the last few centuries.

Political Grace

Welfare

The first challenge to politics is perhaps one of the biggest. Where do we find grace in politics? The Law is prevalent and plentiful in the realm of politics, but where is grace?

Grace is the term that describes what happens when we get what we

---

[118] See John 21:15-17

have not earned and do not deserve. Grace is unfair and unjust. It is an ideal we all seek for ourselves, particularly regarding our debts or misdeeds, but, like the Pharisees, something we rarely desire to give to others.

Economically, we can think of federal and state welfare programs. While we often look at the work of President Franklin D. Roosevelt as the architect of this program in 1935 to help combat the Great Depression our country was in, the actual roots of welfare go back to the British Colonies and their adoption of England's "Poor Laws."[119] For centuries, grace, in the form of welfare programs of a wide variety, has been viewed as an offensive political strategy to combat poverty and the social issues that come with it.

Today, our country has two separate levels of welfare: corporate and individual. Individual welfare has been under attack by conservative politicians for as long as it has been in existence. Their criticisms have focused on the ways that people have used welfare to benefit themselves at the expense of others, when they had the ability to work and contribute themselves. Among the more moderate critics, the problem is typically identified as dependency. Most people do not have major issues helping someone out once, particularly if their misfortune appears to be the result of poor circumstances outside their control. It becomes an issue when they see individuals as repeat clients to the font of grace. The rationale behind this criticism comes in the light of benevolence on behalf of the poor — if the grace is not helping change their circumstances so that they no longer need it, it is not working and should be replaced by something that will keep them from becoming dependents.

Can you imagine how that would work spiritually? How much grace from God would be enough to enable us to "sin no more"?[120] We all become Christ's spiritual dependents for as long as it takes and, if we are honest, though we grow and improve, we are never truly independent of that reliance upon Him.

There is also corporate welfare. In principle, it is the same. Whether it comes in the form of business startup incentives offered through

---

[119] http://www.welfareinfo.org/history/
[120] See John 8:11.

government programs or company bailouts, the concept is grace given in a time of need. Corporations have enjoyed their own form of dependency upon government funds (often in the form of tax breaks) for many years. The rationale behind giving corporations funds has been to help protect the jobs of all those the corporation employs. Sometimes that money gets to the employees. Other times it does not. The same criticism has been applied by different critics as to what to do when grace is misappropriated, or perhaps more accurately, abused.[121]

There are two responses Jesus gives that relate to this. The first one, related directly to giving and serving the needy is, "...freely you have received, freely give.[122]" The second is more directed toward relational grace rather than simple giving. When Peter asked Jesus how many times he should forgive, perhaps up to seven times, Jesus replied that he should forgive seventy times seven.[123] Both passages point to the truth that Jesus calls us to change by giving grace, not by holding back.

One final note on Law and Grace is that they are not mutually exclusive. In fact, the Law of Moses and the Grace of Jesus find fulfillment in one another. "Freely you have received, freely give" is not a new command Jesus made up on the spot. That command is essential to every commandment in the Law of Moses regarding the treatment of orphans, widows, and foreigners. The footnote to each of those commandments is a reminder that God redeemed them from Egypt, giving them grace before they were even given the Law.

> "If among you, one of your brothers should become poor, in any of your towns within your land that the LORD your God is giving you, you shall not harden your heart or shut your hand against your poor brother, but you shall open your hand to him and lend him sufficient for his need, whatever it may be. Take care lest there be an unworthy thought in your heart and you say, 'The seventh year, the year of release is near,' and your eye look grudgingly on your

---

[121] http://www.forbes.com/sites/taxanalysts/2014/03/14/where-is-the-outrage-over-corporate-welfare/#50ee56436881
[122] See Matthew 10:8
[123] See Matthew 18:21-22

poor brother, and you give him nothing, and he cry to the LORD against you, and you be guilty of sin. You shall give to him freely, and your heart shall not be grudging when you give to him, because for this the LORD your God will bless you in all your work and in all that you undertake. For there will never cease to be poor in the land. Therefore, I command you, 'You shall open wide your hand to your brother, to the needy and to the poor, in your land.'

"If your brother, a Hebrew man or a Hebrew woman, is sold to you, he shall serve you six years, and in the seventh year you shall let him go free from you. And when you let him go free from you, you shall not let him go empty-handed. You shall furnish him liberally out of your flock, out of your threshing floor, and out of your winepress. As the LORD your God has blessed you, you shall give to him. You shall remember that you were a slave in the land of Egypt, and the LORD your God redeemed you; therefore, I command you this today.[124]

Frederick Douglas and the Reconstruction

I suspect we would not have become the world power our nation is today were it not for the political grace of Abraham Lincoln and Frederick Douglas. Both men knew the hard life of growing up without power and prestige. They both believed in the importance of education and the power of reason. Perhaps more importantly, both could hold their political power with humility without letting ego, arrogance, or their own high ideals blind them to the reality of life around them.

In Frederick Douglas's address at the second session of the 39th Congress, he advocated for the right to vote for all citizens. While the focus of the day was clearly on the right to vote for all men, his language reflected an appeal for women as well. He had high ideals and was pushing for social changes that would be disruptive in the North as well as in the South. Yet his rationale was simple, elegant, and realistic to the standards and values already held by the entire

---

[124] *The Holy Bible: English Standard Version.* (2001). (Dt 15:7–15). Wheaton: Standard Bible Society.

nation.

Douglas was not asking for special privileges for anyone, regardless of race — nor was he advocating any particular clarification in the constitution made regarding race. He rightly understood the Civil War and the political turmoil of the subsequent Reconstruction as being fought on two separate, but interconnected fronts: Slavery and The Sovereignty of States.

There, before Congress, at the end of the Civil War – in which Douglas was both victim and victor, perhaps the prototype of the redeemed African American man, Douglas could have asked for anything and with the moral privilege of an injured party seeking justice, pushed his way through. Instead of thinking only for himself, he sought the good of all parties involved in the terrible ordeal when he said:

> The Civil Rights Bill and the Freedmen's Bureau Bill and the proposed constitutional amendments, with the amendment already adopted and recognized as the law of the land, do not reach the difficulty, and cannot, unless the whole structure of the government is changed from a government by States to something like a despotic central government, with power to control even the municipal regulations of States, and to make them conform to its own despotic will. While there remains such an idea as the right of each State to control its own local affairs, — an idea, by the way, more deeply rooted in the minds of men of all sections of the country than perhaps any one other political idea, — no general assertion of human rights can be of any practical value. To change the character of the government at this point is neither possible nor desirable. All that is necessary to be done is to make the government consistent with itself, and render the rights of the States compatible with the sacred rights of human nature.[125]

He went on to point out that it was neither profitable nor likely possible to have enough federal government strength to act as a watchdog on every corner, ensuring the compliant behavior of the states. While he stood entirely opposed to slavery, he understood the Rebellion that took place among the southern states was not without its own reasoning and that there was much to be learned by everyone who endured the time of war.

While other politicians were concerned with punishing the South, reappropriating the properties of those who led the Rebellion, and demanding reparations under the banner of "making things right for the evils of slavery," Douglas asked instead for a "clean slate" given to all:

> Without attempting to settle here the metaphysical and somewhat theological question (about which so much has already been said and written), whether once in the Union means always in the Union, — agreeably to the formula, Once in grace always in grace, — it is obvious to common sense that the rebellious States stand to-day, in point of law, precisely where they stood when, exhausted, beaten, conquered, they fell powerless at the feet of Federal authority. Their State governments were overthrown, and the lives and property of the leaders of the Rebellion were forfeited. In reconstructing the institutions of these shattered and overthrown States, Congress should begin with a clean slate, and make clean work of it.[126]

This political grace carried two parts: forgiveness of the past and an establishment of all upon equal footing. Again, Douglas was not proposing a new amendment. He was simply stating that the Constitution of the United States was already written for all citizens — we only needed to be consistent in our use of the law. Here is his closing argument:

> Fortunately, the Constitution of the United States knows no distinction between citizens on account of color. Neither does it know any difference between a citizen of a State and a citizen of the United States. Citizenship evidently includes

---

126

http://www.theatlantic.com/magazine/archive/1866/12/reconstruction/304561

all the rights of citizens, whether State or national. If the Constitution knows none, it is clearly no part of the duty of a Republican Congress now to institute one.[127]

Do our politics exemplify that grace that forgives the past of everyone involved, starting anew with a clean slate? Do they create an environment that places everyone on the same solid ground with one another? Or are we still struggling with these same issues that are rooted in selfishness and personal gain?

Spiritual Authority in Politics

Authority and Responsibility

I think diversity, or difference of opinion, is not only prevalent, but fundamentally necessary in politics. If there were no differences of opinion, there would be no need of government or politics. Diversity is not an enemy. Even as a monotheistic person living in a pluralistic society — pluralism is not the enemy. The temptation to make God in our own image, which is as much idolatry as stone carvings and ritual sacrifices, is the underlying problem in the vast comparisons of religious beliefs today.

The real interactions between sets of values rarely come to the front in our conflicts. Wars have been fought, nations have been conquered, genocides have been justified with strong rallying cries and harsh accusations without ever stating clear values on any side. Many of those wars continue generations after the last shot fired, through the books and media of historical interpretations. These means of keeping the coals warm serve as places where the fighting reignites over time. The world is a mess because we are all a mess.

We have enemies. Our knowledge of each other has grown through the permeation of social media through our cultures, creating new alliances and divisions. What had the potential of being a worldwide "melting pot" has been shifting more and more into something like the alliances that polarized Europe prior to World War I. I'm not sure we should be surprised by this. The myth of the melting pot

---

[127]

http://www.theatlantic.com/magazine/archive/1866/12/reconstruction/304561

never fully came into being and far too often our times of peace have come at the cost of bloodshed to shut out one voice or another. Just as Genesis records, what all too often begins as a lack of respect for boundaries becomes bloodshed in the next generation and outright war in the one after that, and the spirits of those former sins haunt us across time. It is these spirits that Jesus came to save us from. He did so by calling them out for what they were and refusing to let them remain in His presence.

The Zealots wanted freedom, which is another way of saying self-rule. They did not realize that their true enemy lay within themselves, not in Rome. Self-rule is another word for self-control, and the elimination of Rome would not give them any more self-control.

I have noticed that crowds tend to have a high level of reactivity. As long as the crowd believes it is in control, it will be content and stable. It doesn't matter if the crowd is actually in control or not, they only have to perceive that they are. If they perceive that they have lost control though, there will be an immediate reaction to correct that, usually by dominating an external person or group whom they perceive as having authority over them. They seek an external solution to an internal problem

Jesus, on the other hand, had more control over His life than any of us, but He exercised that authority on Himself, through self-control, rather than by taking control of others around Him. In fact, it was His self-control that became a vessel for His authority in the lives of those around Him. He did not go hunting evil spirits, but He did not allow them to exercise their control over Him or those in His presence. Jesus warned that kicking out evil spirits was no guarantee of future freedom.

> "When the unclean spirit has gone out of a person, it passes through waterless places seeking rest, but finds none. Then it says, 'I will return to my house from which I came.' And when it comes, it finds the house empty, swept, and put in order. Then it goes and brings with it seven other spirits more evil than itself, and they enter and dwell there, and the last state of that person is worse than the first. So also will it be with this evil generation.[128]"

---

[128] *The Holy Bible: English Standard Version.* (2001). (Mt 12:43–45). Wheaton: Standard Bible Society.

So, it is only through self-control that we are able to gain freedom, not found through self-rule, but the freedom found through submission to God's rule. We find freedom in following Christ's model of submission to God's authority when He prayed, "nevertheless, not my will, but yours be done.[129]"

Martin Luther King Jr. and Archbishop Oscar Romero

How do we exercise self-control in the presence of our enemies? While I do not believe you must be a pacifist, it may help. The prayer of Saint Francis may be a guide to exercising self-control:

> Lord, make me an instrument of Your peace. Where there is hatred, let me sow love; where there is injury, pardon; where there is doubt, faith; where there is despair, hope; where there is darkness, light; where there is sadness, joy.

> O, Divine Master, grant that I may not so much seek to be consoled as to console; to be understood as to understand; to be loved as to love; For it is in giving that we receive; it is in pardoning that we are pardoned; it is in dying that we are born again to eternal life.[130]

I think the attitude that seeks to understand first before raising a defense protects us from being goaded by spiritual and psychological manipulation that can rob us of the very values we are trying to protect. What is required is not a refusal to defend ourselves, but a refusal of giving up our self-control and our freedom to choose our own responses.

There are several strong examples of political leaders who maintained self-control by advocating non-violent engagement with the society around them. In the United States, one of the most famous examples is Dr. Martin Luther King, Jr. His commitment to non-violence was captivating, even when caught between the instigations of the white supremacists and other political enemies, as well as the mounting pressure from the African American

---

[129] See Luke 22:42 and Matthew 26:42.
[130] http://www.catholic.org/prayers/prayer.php?p=134

community that wanted to use violence to underscore their political statements. Because of this, he gained an authority that has spread across the world regarding political conflict, particularly those involving racial inequality. Rather than fight for a short-term win, Dr. King stood for an ideal that his world could not imagine. Even though that ideal has not yet been realized today, the impact that he made in our nation is visible and his name still carries authority and inspiration to all who hear it today.

Archbishop Oscar Romero was a powerful political figure dealing with enemies outside the United States. His country of El Salvador was caught in a civil war between a corrupt government and a rebellion of the people using guerrilla warfare tactics. Archbishop Romero remained strong in his dedication to non-violence, which allowed him to hold up Christ-like ideals to both the government and the rebels. He was captured and tortured by both sides of the war at different times, but retained his commitment to Christ, and not a political agenda.

Both of these men were assassinated by individuals representing opposing political agendas. Rather than have their lives dictated by the political agendas surrounding them, they lived and led others to live free lives in which they made their own choices. They would not be lured or goaded into giving up their Christian ideals and compromising, even for the sake of saving their own lives.

Political Sacrifice

The Power of Loss and the Hope in Death

Christians are not supposed to hope for death. We are not supposed to even like death. One of the major motivations of becoming a Christian in the first place is to escape death and get eternal life instead. Unfortunately, the idea of escaping death runs completely contrary to the call Jesus gives us to pick up our crosses and follow Him. We are not called to escape death, but to face it knowing Christ has conquered it for us... it has no sting anymore.[131]

With the fear of death comes a hunger for victory and the idea that

---

[131] See 1 Corinthians 15:55-57

we will always win, indeed we *must* always win, because we are the good guys. It strikes me as odd how quickly we can go from proclaiming that our gospel, our *good news* is that we were lost and Christ found us — that we were dead, but in Christ we have found new life — to a message that proclaims that *we* must conquer so Christ will be glorified, or that *we* must ensure our future or else the salvation of our world will be lost. Contrary to popular belief, common sense, or our gut feelings, there is power to be found in losing.

In the tribal cultures, particularly in ancient times, the political losers were often killed outright. Whether this was an individual who was a rival for leadership, or a nation of people competing over common resources, there was no concept of "live and let live." This prevented the possibility of a comeback assault at a later date. As nations grew, some of them began to enslave the nations they dominated. While this may have been a more merciful act, those slave nations often banded together to attack the dominant culture, just as those who executed their enemies had feared.

The Jews came from a place of slavery in Egypt until about 1300 BC when God delivered them from Pharaoh. 40 years later, they became a nation and began conquering, destroying, and, in some cases, enslaving other nations. They rose to the height of their political power just after 1000 BC but civil war weakened them and it was not long before Northern Israel and finally Judah in the south both were conquered, exiled, and enslaved again. 1000 years later, during the time of Jesus, I think too few Jews fully understood the leverage they had toward the bottom of the social ladder.

What leverage? The power gained by holding everyone else up. In most societies, the common-born, least educated people do the work that no one else wants to do but is essential to the maintenance of the society. In the United States, this level is made up of immigrants, those with criminal records, and minority cultures (ethnic or economic) who do not have easy access to education or well paying job networks. These people make up the bulk of our agriculture, food service, hospitality, and low-level medical aid workforce. Imagine what would happen to our country if all these people stopped working and moved away. Farms would have rotting produce and starving livestock, with no one willing to help. Restaurants all over would close due to lack of workers and lack of food to sell. Hotels would shut down and travelers would have nowhere to stay. Hospitals would have to turn people away for lack of service available. How long would our nation last if that happened? A month? A week? The majority of people are not prepared to grow their own food, nor do they have access to the resources or skills to do so. Losing all of those people at once would be a nightmare from which we might never recover.

Not only do we need those workers, but our society needs them to work hard for little pay. If we paid people according to amount of energy spent instead of amount of education, skill, and personal networking, most of us could still not afford those basic needs. Those workers hold our nation in the palm of their hand, and the only thing that holds them back is a lack of ownership. Since they do not own the property they work or the products they make, they cannot exercise power by gaining more work or more pay. The power they wield across our nation is when they are willing to lose their job and stop production. Perhaps this is why so many corporations have taken their businesses out of the country to places either where low wages are more acceptable socially and work can be enforced more, or where the inflation rate is such that the low wages they pay end up being decent wages in those countries.

Civil rights movements throughout history have understood this concept of the power of losing and used it to make changes in the culture surrounding them. The most successful movements have truly been populated by the poor of the society, as opposed to middle- and lower-middle class people pretending to be poor. The more personal investment you have in the political and economic systems in place, the more power it has over you and the less freedom you have to change it. Those who have nothing to lose, because they have already lost everything, have the most power to truly change the world around them.

George Washington

How does that look on an individual level? Consider George Washington's example. After leading the colonists to victory over the British in the Revolutionary War, the founders of the constitution began to set up a democracy and started bidding for political power. Those soldiers and the people wanted a leader they could trust, though, and George Washington accepted the first Presidency of the United States of America. He was more military leader and man of the people than politician, however, and, after serving two four-year terms, he stepped down from office and entered retirement. In doing so, he set the precedent for every president after him to only run for two terms, which was officially made into law after Franklin D. Roosevelt served four terms during the Great Depression and World War II.

Here is what made Washington unique. There was no precedent before him and he could have served out the remainder of his life as President. In fact, following the Revolutionary War, many of the people wanted to scrap the Constitution and just crown him King of the United States. He held all the power, and his time as president only added to that respect and reverence. He understood, though, that although the people believed they would be happy with him as king, it would hurt the country in the long run. Indeed, having the same leader for too many years was too close to having a king in practice if not in name. So he decided to step down. In stepping down from that power, he gained even more credibility. He wielded power by giving it up.

How so? Even in his retirement, Washington could have walked up to congress, or the new president, and turned the political tides — even without his title. The president who followed him knew that every day he held office was only because Washington allowed him to, by giving it up himself. There was no contest there. Washington had decided to move on to better things than the Presidency of the United States, and, in doing so, unintentionally elevated himself above all the politicians of his day, and ours as well. He will forever be known as one of the best presidents of this country, not for what he did in office, but for what he did before he held office, and the way he let his office go.

Murder or Sacrifice

Throughout history, many leaders have used the concept of sacrifice to encourage or command others to give up their lives in order to preserve the leader's own authority. This is not sacrifice, this is murder. This is the same concept that God spoke against when He prohibited the rituals the Canaanite cultures called "child sacrifice".[132] Those who practiced such "sacrifice" were condemned and put to death as murderers. This twisted concept of sacrifice is also the same spirit that led the Jewish leaders to crucify Jesus.[133] In this instance, it is God making the sacrifice to the people, not the people sacrificing something to God. True sacrifice is always done by the person in power, for the benefit of those they lead.

In our troubling and turbulent times, it needs to be stated that there is a difference between murder and sacrifice. War has probably changed more in the last 100 years than in all the years leading up to the twentieth century combined. We went from guns and horses to gas and tanks, to bombs and planes, to nuclear missiles, germ warfare, and, in recent decades, an increased recruitment of civilians turned into suicidal weapons of mass destruction themselves. Our War against Terrorism has us looking suspiciously at everyone around us, and not without cause.

Whether it is Syrian refugees, African American Muslims, White Supremacists, Hispanic drug cartels, Asian human trafficking... there is no racial profile that does not carry with it connections to violence. The mass violence that was once linked primarily with drug use and history of mental illness is now being connected with political views. The killings are done to get media attention and any death the perpetrators face is seen as bringing honor to their cause or group. At least that is what some of these people believe.

In reality though, the names of those murder-suicides do not last. The names of their victims and the heroes who gave their lives trying to rescue the victims in these terrorist attacks will long outlive the violent offenders. Even more, these terrorist groups are now in competition with one another for media time and it seems they now are common enough to have lost much of their unique, almost celebrity status. They are just another one of those people, and their political voice is being drowned out by the ripples of violence they

---

[132] Leviticus 20:2-5
[133] John 11:49-50

have created. This is certainly not a Christian concept of sacrifice, nor does it work. Christian sacrifice means willingness to give your life in order to save a life, not in order to take life. Murder-suicide should never be considered Christian sacrifice. Bringing death upon others does not gain you political power — saving their lives does.

Faith at Work in Politics

Mother Teresa, the politician

Very few people have ever reached the level of political influence as someone like Mother Teresa. The levels of political influence typically start in local communities — maybe even leadership in a church congregation. From there any person may potentially grow into city, county, state, and, if they work hard, perhaps national leadership. The amount of wealth you work with and have access to grows with each of these promotions, as does the responsibility. This ladder of politics remains pretty consistent, and I expect most countries have similar political processes of advancement.

There is a difference when you reach the level of international leadership, though. It can be done with hard work and a lot of money, and many have done it, but leadership done solely through financial power is a tenuous grasp that only holds as long as the economy flows to your benefit. Those who attain a status as an international leader and especially those who hold it are rare and unique, and while international status gives a person access to tremendous amounts of wealth, many of the greatest international leaders did not use that wealth themselves.

Consider the example of Mother Teresa.[134] She was born Gonxha Agnes Bojaxhiu, coming from a family in Albania who faced financial struggle after losing her father when she was only 8 years old. When she turned 18, she joined the Sisters of Loreto in Ireland, following her call to mission work, and a year later she arrived in Calcutta, India. Mother Teresa spent her life caring for the sick and dying of the poorest of the poor in our world, and it was this service and witness of the love of God that gradually brought the world to

---

[134] http://www.motherteresa.org/layout.html

her doorstep. Politicians come and go. As long as there are seats of power, there will be people to fill them. Leaders, especially ones who live out their faith in service to others, are a different story.

Mother Teresa lived out the gospel message with her life and service to others, offering that message of love and hope to those who could not read it themselves. This is at the heart of incarnational life and ministry. She was able to be deep *in* the heart of the world without being *of* the world or overly influenced *by* the world. Her hope rested securely in God, not in what those she served could do for her. That was her strength. She could give without taking. In giving up her life to service, she was able to become a fountain of blessing that transformed every life that touched hers. She gained political authority, not through any process of election, for there was not seat of power for her to occupy.

Instead, she caught the attention of the world by bringing hope and dignity into places that our world politics could not or would not touch, and, in doing so, she created a new kind of political authority. When the people with whom she served had no voice in politics, she became their voice. The political authorities might not hear the forgotten and nameless, dying in poverty, but they knew the voice of Mother Teresa and she could hold them accountable because she was actively making a difference herself. She was, in her own way, competition for the hearts and minds of people in the world.

Living faith out in public

One of the most famous lines in the letter of James, found in the New Testament, says, "Faith without works is dead.[135]" There is probably still a small amount of discussion today about whether you can be a Christian without works, although I suspect most of this discussion has been settled in the scripture itself. However, the discussions that are alive and well on this subject are what things count as "works" that make faith alive.

It is almost always easier perform such "works" of faith within your own local community, for the benefit of those most like you. By contrast however, Jesus commands us to love, not just our friends,

---

but our enemies as well.[136] This is one such "work" of faith that has challenged believers since the day Jesus first taught it.

At the same time, there has been a parting of ways within the church that goes back, probably to a time even before Jesus. The same notion the Essenes had, that it was better, or at least easier, to follow God outside the everyday life found in the cities and civic communities in the world. Their answer has been to form new communities, based solely on worshiping and serving God. They exist today in the many monastic movements and populated by those who forsake the world, their families, and the opportunities they may have had there, and join with a monastery or convent to live a life dedicated to God.

This same movement continues today, even among those outside the Roman Catholic faith in new ways, new monastic communities. It appears in Christian private schools and a growing movement of Christian homeschooling parents. There are also new churches started in specific neighborhoods, created for the people among their properties, as a means of taking back parts of cities for God.[137] There is good found in all of these movements, yet there remains the temptation to create our own Christian cave to hide away from the world.

The critics of these movements point out that we cannot be witnesses of Christ to our world and fulfill the great commission by hiding away and only interacting with other Christians. Jesus Himself pointed out that a light is not made to be hidden under a bowl, but is to be uncovered to share the light all around.[138] It should also be noted that a candle or oil lamp (the kinds of light used in Jesus day) would eventually suffocate under that bowl and be snuffed out. These critics rightly show that there is something essential to a living and growing faith that requires engagement with the parts of the world that do not follow God.

Does this mean that you cannot be a monastic and have a living

---

[136] Matthew 5:43-48

[137] http://www.new-monastics.com/

[138] See Matthew 5:15

faith? Absolutely not! We have already seen how Mother Teresa had a foot firmly in both of those worlds, and it was because of that stance that she was able to be the incarnational gift our world needed so much. To live that incarnate life, we just have to ask ourselves where our own footing is. Where is our foundation, upon which we find our support, and where is our mission field, where we let our faith shine?

Parting Challenges

Jesus never promised it would be easy

Our call to discipleship is to pick up our cross and follow Jesus. That call carries its own cost to us. The cross, in which we see our hope and salvation, was a symbol of torment and death for Jesus, and so our own crosses lay a claim upon our lives. Jesus never promised that life following Him would be easy or comfortable, and certainly not in the area of politics.

Political grace, as tame as this term sounds, costs us our plans and ambitions. One of the greatest examples of political and economic grace is found in Leviticus 25: the year of Jubilee. Once, every 50 years, the Jews were to let all property revert back to their original owners. All debts were canceled that year, no matter how much you owed or when you took that loan out. Everybody in society had their slate wiped clean and had to start from scratch. That sounds wonderful for those who had fallen into bad times, but what about those who were close to or in their retirement? How could they be expected to give up all for which they had spent so many years working? It is curious to note that there is no evidence that Israel ever celebrated this 50th year of Jubilee, even though it was written in their Law. Yet this is the first thing that Jesus preached in his hometown, as foretold in Isaiah, proclaiming that this year of grace had come at last.[139]

Spiritual Authority and self-control are difficult enough to manage in times of peace, but what about in times of war? Today in particular, wars are being fought across continents with unrecognized political entities who may not have a seat in the United

---

[139] See Luke 4:14-30

Nations, but still have powerful political sway in many countries today. Should we be surprised? I think they may have learned politics from the Christian movement, who started as a group of unknown people, scattered across a handful of nations in the Middle East and southern Europe, and whose leader (the Pope) rose to become the one who crowned kings and manipulated political agendas up through the nineteenth century, and still influences politics today.

I wish I could say the difference is the violence our new competitors bring, but in truth, the Church has turned to violence at times in our own history to accomplish our own ends. No, in these days it is not easy keeping our spiritual and political priorities in line, dealing with the root spiritual causes that break out in political messes and violence. This kind of authority, rooted in self-control, costs us our safety as we step out into danger, unarmed and defenseless, in order to bring down the walls built up against the love and grace of God.

Political sacrifice means giving up the power to control the politics in our own communities. It means being willing to step down when the choice is compromising our values. Would you be willing to resign from your job if your supervisor demanded you to do something against your faith and ideals? As much as we sometimes spin the news like the Zealots, worrying about the day when Christian persecution will break out in this country, our more immediate threat is the one the Sadducees faced: loss of Christian leaders in government and consequently a loss of economic power.

The sad truth is, churches are closing every day, not because the government is prohibiting them from preaching and teaching, but simply because they cannot pay the bills. Somewhere in our past, the devil started a boycott of church that is still going on today, and now, with a greater number of non-Christians in our nation, it is those outside the faith that are elected to political offices. The question we face today is: what will we compromise to keep the institution of the church up and running? What beliefs, doctrines, or behaviors will we tolerate to gain us a few more years? Or, on the other hand, are we willing to sacrifice this institution of the church, let it be torn down with no bricks left upon one another, paved over and turned into commercial real estate — with the expectation that in three days' time God will raise it up again? Do we believe in the resurrection of the Church? Do we believe that where we fail, fall, and are buried in the earth, God will raise us up to new life?

It is easy to want to find a place to hide out until all this comes to pass. After all, it is not by our own strength that anything will be accomplished for God's kingdom. But this is precisely the attitude that shuts down the Church. The Church does not exist in walls of a building or services held on a particular day of the week. The Church exists wherever there are people who are willing to follow Christ, regardless of the cost, and to step up and step out to share the message that our world needs to hear. He is alive! Jesus Christ lives today! I've walked with Him and talked with Him and He helped me on the way! I've seen Him at work in my life and I see Him at work in your life as well. Let me introduce you to the Savior of the world, the God who never rests, who never gives up, who overcomes by stepping up to the gates of Hell and knocking the doors down with but a word. This is God's Word that created the world and became flesh, who lived among us and served us, who died in our place and whom death could not hold. Here is His Spirit that He shares with us, that holds us together along the Way, the Life, and the Truth. This is what I value more than life itself, and it cannot be taken from me. This grace, this life, this love I share now with you.

Brothers and sisters, this is the reason we were created: to receive the love of God and to share it with everyone we meet. If God leads you into the political arena, giving you responsibility over hundreds or thousands, sharing His love among them is still your purpose in life. If you stand on the fringes of society and have no political voice, sharing that love of God with whomever you meet is still your purpose. God wants His love shared among Democrats and Republicans alike, among libertarians and anarchists, among the kings and the slaves of the earth, and then, at the end of the day, we will see that all of this mess, all of this tension, all the hurt and scandal and strife, has been in His hands the whole time.

9 781949 888485